The Seminole Indians of Florida

Southeastern Classics in Archaeology,

Anthropology, and History

D1522488

Southeastern Classics in Archaeology, Anthropology, and History

Jerald T. Milanich, Series Editor

Each volume in this series represents nineteenth- and twentieth-century scholarly works
still used today by students of the Native American societies of the southeastern
United States and the colonial period.

Archeology of the Florida Gulf Coast, by Gordon R. Willey
The Early History of the Creek Indians and Their Neighbors, by John R. Swanton
Space and Time Perspective in Northern St. Johns Archeology, Florida,
by John M. Goggin
Famous Florida Sites: Crystal River and Mount Royal, edited by Jerald T. Milanich
Here They Once Stood: The Tragic End of the Apalachee Missions,
by Mark F. Boyd, Hale G. Smith, and John W. Griffin
Exploration of Ancient Key-Dweller Remains on the Gulf Coast of Florida,
by Frank Hamilton Cushing
Exploration of the Etowah Site in Georgia: The Etowah Papers,
by Warren King Moorehead
The Seminole Indians of Florida, by Clay MacCauley

The Seminole Indians
of Florida

———◆———

Clay MacCauley

with a new introduction by William C. Sturtevant

foreword by Jerald T. Milanich, series editor

University Press of Florida

Gainesville · Tallahassee · Tampa · Boca Raton

Pensacola · Orlando · Miami · Jacksonville · Ft. Myers

Copyright 2000 by the Board of Regents of the State of Florida
Printed in the United States of America on acid-free paper
All rights reserved
12 11 10 09 08 07 7 6 5 4 3 2
Library of Congress Cataloging-in-Publication Data

MacCauley, Clay, 1843–1925.
The Seminole Indians of Florida / Clay MacCauley; with a new introduction by
William C. Sturtevant; foreword by Jerald T. Milanich.
p. cm. – (Southeastern classics in archaeology, anthropology, and history)
Includes bibliographical references.
ISBN 0-8130-1792-0 (pbk.: alk. paper)
1. Seminole Indians–History. 2. Seminole Indians–Social life and customs.
I. Title. II. Series.
E51.U55 5th
[E99.S28 b M2]
975.9004'973–dc21   00-036404

The University Press of Florida is the scholarly publishing agency for the State
University System of Florida, comprising Florida A&M University, Florida Atlantic
University, Florida Gulf Coast University, Florida International University, Florida
State University, University of Central Florida, University of Florida, University of
North Florida, University of South Florida, and University of West Florida.

University Press of Florida
15 Northwest 15th Street
Gainesville, FL 32611–2079
http://www.upf.com

CONTENTS

FOREWORD

What makes a classic? Why are some books and articles as useful today as when they were first written? For archaeologists, anthropologists, and historians interested in the Native American cultures of the southeastern United States and the events of the colonial period, classics are references that contain ideas and knowledge essential to research. Some classics helped to shape a field of study, while others helped in the development of the fundamental taxonomies in use today, and still others offer basic building blocks of information that can be used to create theoretical models. Many classics exhibit all of these characteristics. These are indeed publications that active researchers cannot live without.

On my own shelves are a number of classics, and I consult them frequently. They are the books my students covet, and I guard them zealously, for scholarly as well as financial reasons. Classics—if one can still find them at all—can cost a pretty penny!

The knowledge published in classics endures through the ages, but the physical books themselves are often less fortunate. Originally published in paperback with non-acid-free pages and bindings, in limited printings or in hard-to-find journals, some of them have become rare indeed.

The *Southeastern Classics* series puts back into print books and articles deemed by scholars to be timeless treasures, resources that we all use but that are difficult or impossible to find. As someone who has always loved books and could not wait for the Bookmobile to visit my neighborhood during the summers of my youth, I am very pleased to be a part of this project.

Clay MacCauley's 1887 *The Seminole Indians of Florida* is a classic. It was originally published in the Fifth Annual Report of the Smithsonian Institution's Bureau of Ethnology; it is reproduced in the present volume from the original and thus retains its original pagination in the report (beginning on page 471). In his account MacCauley fashioned an informative snapshot of the Seminole people at a time when their way of life was little known to the rest of the world.

Supplementing Clay MacCauley's report are an introduction and supplementary materials (photographs and a census of the Seminoles, the latter made by MacCauley) provided by William C. Sturtevant, curator and ethnologist in the Department of Anthropology at the Smithsonian Institution's National Museum of Natural History. (That department is the successor to the Bureau of Ethnology, later the Bureau of American Ethnology.) William Sturtevant is recognized as the world's leading scholar on the Seminole and he has published widely on the Seminole and other Native Americans. His contributions enhance Clay MacCauley's report, making it an even more valuable resource for learning about the Seminole and Miccosukee Indians of Florida.

Jerald T. Milanich
Series Editor

INTRODUCTION

WILLIAM C. STURTEVANT

In 1879 Congress passed an act providing for special censuses of "all Indians not taxed," and the acquisition of "such information as to their conditions as may be obtainable." Major J. W. Powell, head of the Bureau of [American] Ethnology, founded in the same year, was appointed "a Special Agent of the Census Bureau to prepare schedules and superintend this work, with Colonel Garrick Mallery and Messrs. H. W. Henshaw, S. D. Hinman, R. L. Packard, and Clay McCauley as assistants" (Marble 1880). Powell may well have lobbied Congress for this act, in order to use Census Bureau funding to support the ethnographic research his bureau was initiating. And all those named as his assistants became staff members or collaborators of the Bureau of Ethnology for other projects. The phrase requiring the census takers among the Indians to collect information "as to their conditions" also hints at Powell's involvement.

A letter of September 15, 1880, from Clay MacCauley in Roxbury, Massachusetts, to Major Powell clearly indicates that he was already on the bureau staff, as he awaited a copy of Powell's *Introduction to the Study of Indian Languages* (Powell 1880) while he read "Spencer's volume on sociology" (probably Spencer 1874, not a favorite of Powell's—see Hinsley 1981:127). MacCauley was assigned to supervise the census of the Indians east of the Mississippi. In the autumn of 1880 he began with the Ojibwa and Menomini reservations in Minnesota and Wisconsin. In addition to the censuses, he conducted ethnographic inquiries, sending to Powell from the Green Bay Agency a list of the Menomini "gentes" (MacCauley 1880b), writing up his findings on the Menomini Dream Dance, and also submitting a report on the Ojibwa. He then visited the Eastern Cherokee in North Carolina. However, his principal task was "to enquire particularly into the condition, manners and customs, and other interests of the Florida Seminole" (MacCauley 1914: 265–82).

In his annual reports for the fiscal years 1879–83, Powell does not mention the Indian census work. However, in the Second Annual Report he alludes to the ethnological work of three of the five men assigned to the special Indian census: "Mr. W. W. Henshaw spent a large part of the year in personal examination of the tribes of the Pacific slope, including those of Washington Territory, Rev. S. D. Hinman visited the Dakotas, and Rev. Clay MacCauley, besides reporting upon the Ojibwas, made the first ethnologic exploration of the Seminoles of Florida ever successfully attempted" (Powell 1883b: xxv).

MacCauley's Florida work was accomplished during January, February, and March 1881; his census sheets are dated February and March 1881. On returning to Washington, he submitted a copy of Powell's linguistic questionnaire fully filled out, with a few ethnographic notes on the final pages (MacCauley 1881a). The verb paradigms are especially complete. The language is Creek, not Mikasuki, the latter being the first language of Billy Conepatchie (spelled Ko-nip-ha-tco by MacCauley)— that is, Little Billie of the Wind Clan, whose Mikasuki name was *koniphá:ci* (in Creek *ko:naphá:co*), and who was MacCauley's interpreter and principal informant.

On May 3, 1881, MacCauley read a paper at a meeting of the Anthropological Society of Washington, entitled "The Personal Characteristics of the Seminole Indians" (ASW 1879–83), no doubt comparable to the similarly titled section on pages 481–94 of his published report. However, the full report, reprinted in the present volume, was long in coming. Although it was planned for the Second Annual Report of the Bureau of Ethnology, which was issued in 1883, it was not published until 1887 in the Fifth Annual Report. On June 13, 1881, he sent the bureau "sketches for wood-cuts, to be used in illustrating the report upon the Florida Seminoles, which I am now preparing." The accompanying letter is endorsed on the back: "22 sketches sent to the Public Printer June 18/81, to be reproduced by Nichols for 2d. An. Rep. Bu. of Ethnology" (MacCauley 1881b). The report as published has only sixteen woodcuts (plus one map and one plan). It also has an engraving of Key West Billy (Fig. 62), based on a photograph that MacCauley sent on July 1, 1881 (MacCauley 1881c; see Fig. 1 in the photo section following this introduction). The sketches (for which the originals have not been located) were probably made by Lt. E. T. Brown, who accompanied MacCauley on his visit to the Cat Fish Lake settlement (MacCauley 1887: 489–91) and who did the drawings for R. H. Pratt's report on his visit to the Seminoles the year before (reproduced in Sturtevant 1956).

There was then a delay. MacCauley later explained that he suffered a "break down" in the spring of 1881, perhaps contracted malaria in Florida (which seems unlikely), and had to stop all his work (MacCauley 1914: 290–91; 1882a). He spent the winter of 1881–82 in Italy, then went to Montana to recuperate further before returning east to Minneapolis, where he spent 1884–89 as a newspaper writer, preacher, and lecturer. Thus goes MacCauley's account in his autobiography; however, on October 12, 1882, he wrote to Powell from New Ipswich, New Hampshire, saying he had been unable to work the previous summer but that now "life begins again to wear a cheerful look," and that he planned to return to Washington in November (MacCauley 1882b). But on January 9, 1883, Powell wrote to MacCauley (in care of A. D. Chandler in Boston), rather coldly informing him that his employment at the Bureau of Ethnology was terminated because the Census Bureau had cut off funding, as of January 10, for Powell's work on the census.

It is not clear when MacCauley's Seminole manuscript was finally submitted for publication. Powell's letter of transmittal for the Fifth Annual Report, in which it was published in 1887, is dated October 25, 1884.

How Powell found MacCauley for work on the census and for ethnographic fieldwork in Florida is unknown. Furthermore, there is no indication of MacCauley's interest in American Indians (or in the nascent field of anthropology) either before or after his work for Powell, although he did say that he was influenced by his boyhood readings of Elisha Kent Kane on the Arctic and of accounts of Commodore Perry's expedition to Japan (MacCauley 1914: 23).

MacCauley was born in 1843 in Chambersburg, Pennsylvania, to a Scotch-Irish family—which may explain his changing the spelling of his surname from McCauley to (a more Scottish?) MacCauley. He first studied for the ministry at Dickinson College, a Methodist school in Carlisle, Pennsylvania, where he joined the student militia and enlisted in the army after hearing Abraham Lincoln speak. But he was soon discharged as a minor, and entered Princeton College as a junior in 1861. In 1862 he re-enlisted in the army and was captured by Stonewall Jackson in the Battle of Chancellorsville, Virginia, and sent to Libby Prison. Paroled home, he re-entered Princeton and graduated in 1864. He then alternated theological training in Allegheny, Pennsylvania, and Chicago with summer service in army hospitals, leaving the army at the end of the Civil War.

Serving as first a Presbyterian and then a Congregationalist minister, he finally joined the Unitarians and became minister of a Unitarian church in Detroit, then in Rochester, New York, and finally in Waltham, Massachusetts. He resigned in 1873 and went to Heidelberg, Leipzig, and Dresden to study philosophy and theology. Returning from Germany in 1875, he became minister of the First Unitarian Church (later All Souls Church) in Washington, D.C., from 1877 until he resigned as of September 30, 1880—ostensibly because of ill health, but in fact due to a disagreement over church finances (MacCauley 1914; Wildes 1933).

At this point MacCauley was at loose ends, until "some friends arranged to have [him] undertake special service for the Bureau of Ethnology of the Smithsonian Institution" (MacCauley 1914: 265). No doubt this was Major Powell's doing, although he is not credited in the autobiography.

After Powell dismissed him from the Bureau of Ethnology in 1883, MacCauley moved to Minneapolis and St. Paul. Finally in 1889 he found his calling, serving until he retired in 1920 as a member or director of the Unitarian mission in Japan. He died in Berkeley, California, in 1925.

MacCauley published a great deal, especially during his years in Tokyo, in both English and Japanese, on Christianity, philosophy, history, his memories of the Civil War, and on English and Japanese literature—thirty-nine titles are listed in the National Union Catalog. Among these works was *An Introductory Course in Japanese*, (Yokohama, 1896, reprinted in 1897 and 1906), a book of 569 pages from which an *Outline of Japanese Grammar* (111 pages) was extracted for a separate printing in 1938 by the Department of Oriental Languages, University of California, Berkeley, reprinted in 1942 by another publisher. I have not examined these works, but none of the titles—except for the work here reprinted—implies any interest in anthropology or American Indians.

MacCauley's investigation of Seminole culture is one of the earliest examples of serious ethnological fieldwork supported by the Bureau of American Ethnology. Frank Hamilton Cushing's work among the Zuni began in 1879 and lasted much longer than MacCauley's, but did not result in a published general ethnography. In 1878 Powell had sent J. Owen Dorsey to conduct fieldwork among the Omaha; he was a former missionary, already very knowledgeable about Siouan languages and cultures, who had wide interests and took thorough notes (Hinsley 1981: 174). His "Omaha Sociology," published in the Third Annual Report of the bureau (Dorsey 1884), is much longer and more detailed than MacCauley's Seminole report, but the topics investigated and the order in which they are presented closely resemble those in MacCauley's report. The implication is strong that an outline provided by Powell underlies both MacCauley's and Dorsey's ethnographies. This is also suggested by the fact that some sections of MacCauley's report are very brief, and some of his headings are followed by comments to the effect that he could acquire little or no information on those topics.

Whatever the influences behind his work, MacCauley's short Seminole monograph is remarkably good for its time in both the breadth and depth of its coverage, despite the real difficulties that other sources indicate he must have faced in acquiring the information. The monograph is still useful for an understanding of Florida Seminole and Miccosukee culture.

Note

I thank Sally McLendon for much help with research during our fieldwork in south Florida in January, 2000, and for a great deal of editorial assistance, especially with the illustrations and the census.

Works Cited

Anthropological Society of Washington (ASW)
1879–83. Minutes of 39th Meeting, May 3, 1881. MS 4821, Box 2, Anthropological Society of Washington, Box 2, Series 2. National Anthropological Archives, Smithsonian Institution, Washington, D.C.

Dorsey, J. Owen
1884. Omaha Sociology. In *Third Annual Report of the Bureau of [American] Ethnology to the Secretary of the Smithsonian Institution, 1881–82*, pp. 211–370. Washington, D.C.: Government Printing Office.

Hinsley, Curtis M., Jr.
1981. *Savages and Scientists: The Smithsonian Institution and the Development of American Anthropology 1846–1910*. Washington, D.C.: Smithsonian Institution Press.

MacCauley, Clay
1880a. Letter to Maj. J.W. Powell, from Roxbury, Mass., September 15, 1880. MS, BAE Correspondence, Letters Received, 1879–1888, National Anthropological Archives, Smithsonian Institution, Washington, D.C.

1880b. Letter to Maj. J. W. Powell, with list of Menomini gentes, from Green Bay Agency, Keehena, Wis., November 1, 1880. MS, 2 pp., BAE MS 59, National Anthropological Archives, Smithsonian Institution, Washington, D.C.

1881a. Copy of Powell 1880, filled out for the Florida Seminole Indians. BAE MS 589, National Anthropological Archives, Smithsonian Institution, Washington, D.C.

1881b. Letter to Maj. J. W. Powell, from Washington, D.C., June 13, 1881. MS, BAE Correspondence, Letters Received, 1879–88, National Anthropological Archives, Smithsonian Institution, Washington, D.C.

1881c. Letter to Maj. J. W. Powell, from Roxbury, Mass., July 1, 1881. MS, BAE Correspondence, Letters Received, 1879–88, National Anthropological Archives, Smithsonian Institution, Washington D.C.

1882a. Letter to J. C. Pilling, from Naples, Italy, February 24, 1882. MS,

BAE Correspondence, Letters Received, 1879–88, National Anthropological Archives, Smithsonian Institution, Washington, D.C.

1882b. Letter to Maj. J. W. Powell, from New Ipswich, N.H., October 12, 1882. MS, BAE Correspondence, Letters Received, 1879–88, National Anthropological Archives, Smithsonian Institution, Washington, D.C.

1887. The Seminole Indians of Florida. In *Fifth Annual Report of the Bureau of [American] Ethnology to the Secretary of the Smithsonian Institution, 1883–84*, pp. 469–531. Washington, D.C.: Government Printing Office.

1914. *Memories and Memorials: Gatherings from an Eventful Life.* Tokyo: n.p.

Marble, E. M., Acting Commissioner of Indian Affairs

1880. Circular no. 56. Office of Indian Affairs, Washington, D.C. Copy in Kiowa Agency Records, Oklahoma Historical Society, microfilm roll KA 1-A, frame 12. Copy provided by Thomas W. Kavanagh.

Powell, John Wesley

1880. *Introduction to the Study of Indian Languages, with Words, Phrases, and Sentences to be Collected.* 2nd ed., with charts. Washington, D.C.: Government Printing Office.

1883a. Letter to Clay MacCauley, January 9, 1883. MS, BAE Correspondence, Letters Sent, 1879–1888, National Anthropological Archives, Smithsonian Institution, Washington, D.C.

1883b. Second Annual Report of the Bureau of Ethnology to the Secretary of the Smithsonian Institution, 1880–81, pp. xv–xxxvii. Washington, D.C.: Government Printing Office.

Spencer, Herbert

1874. *The Study of Sociology.* New York: Appleton.

Sturtevant, William C., ed. and annotator.

1956. R. H. Pratt's Report on the Seminole in 1879. *Florida Anthropologist* 9(1): 1–24.

Wildes, Harry Emerson

1933. MacCauley, Clay. Vol. 11 of *Dictionary of American Biography*, ed. Dumas Malone, pp. 572–73. New York: Charles Scribner's Sons.

Late Nineteenth-Century Photographs
of Seminole Indians

MacCauley's report was published before the Smithsonian Institution could adequately reproduce photographs. Many of the people recorded in the census had been, or would be, photographed during the 1880s and 1890s. Following are twenty photographs of Seminoles taken about the time of MacCauley's visit, gathered from various archives and captioned partly

Figure 1. "Key West Billy" (Billy Fewell, *hotalkihâ:ci*, Wind Clan, Mikasuki), photographed at least six years before MacCauley's visit in 1881. This is a heavily retouched photograph, used to make the engraving published in MacCauley's report (Fig. 62, p. 484). Key West Billy was the older brother of Little Billie and the head of household #7 at Big Cypress. MacCauley describes the source of his English name (pp. 484–85). In 1881 Key West Billy was unique among the Seminoles in having built a two-story cypress board house with windows, door, and balcony (p. 501). Here he wears many Seminole-made silver ornaments: turban band, four gorgets, and two bracelets (p. 489). The skirt of his coat has appliqué decoration, and he has a beaded sash over his left shoulder, with braided fringes tied on his right hip. The flaps of his leggings have been narrowed by retouching. (National Anthropological Archives, Smithsonian Institution, neg. 44–262-C.)

on the basis of consultation with well-informed Seminoles in the early
1950s and more briefly in January 2000. The Indian names are spelled
according to their pronunciation in the Mikasuki language.

Figure 2. "Key West Billy" (Billy Fewell, *hotalkihâ:ci*, Wind Clan, Mikasuki), in a
studio photograph taken on the same occasion as Fig. 1. It is not clear which print has
been laterally reversed. Here his buckskin moccasins and leggings are well shown. This
photograph—and thus the other one—was taken in 1874 or before (perhaps during his
trip to Key West), because it was received in that year by the predecessor of the Musée de
l'Homme, Paris. (Photothèque, Musée de l'Homme, Paris, print 44−9803−173.)

Figure 3. Young Seminole man (unidentified). Photograph copied from a hand-tinted tintype taken by Charles H. Stephens in Florida in 1876. The feathers in the turban were added in the early retouching. (National Anthropological Archives, Smithsonian Institution, neg. 45,119.)

Figure 4. Members of a Creek Seminole family in their best dress, about 1887. *Left to right:* "Chief" Tallahassee, *fŏstastanakô:ci,* of family #35 at Cat Fish Lake (see MacCauley's report, pp. 491, 502); his sister's daughter Martha Tiger and her daughter Emma Osceola of the Cat Fish Lake family #34; Tallahassee's youngest son Tommy Hill, "Ya-wi-lai-yi," Deer Clan, of family 34; and Lucy Gopher, *omalâyki,* another daughter of Martha Tiger. All except Tommy Hill were of the Creek Seminole Little Bird Clan. Only Lucy Gopher was still living in 1953, on the Brighton Reservation. The group stands before a palmetto-thatched temporary structure at their camp on a shell mound on the south shore of Lake Hutchineha. Tallahassee wears a beaded pouch and sash, with a woven sash over his left shoulder. The women wear heavy bead necklaces (typical of the time) and many silver brooches attached to their capes. Martha Tiger holds a Seminole-made basket. MacCauley met Tallahassee and his sons camping at the koonti grounds on Horse Creek; Fig. 67 in his report shows Tallahassee's temporary shelter there (p. 502). The photograph was probably taken by J. M. Willson, Jr. (National Anthropological Archives, Smithsonian Institution, 1178-N-1.)

Figure 5. kasá:yi, Otter Clan, Mikasuki, wife of Cypress Charlie, Big Cypress family#12, about 1886 at Coconut Grove, where Big Cypress and Miami River families came to trade and visit, camping on Munroe's waterfront. She wears the multiple-strand bead necklaces that were typical well into the twentieth century, with suspended silver disks (see MacCauley's Fig. 63 and pp. 487–488). Her arms cover her bare midriff, as most Seminole women posed when being photographed during this period. Photograph by Ralph Middleton Munroe. (Historical Association of Southern Florida, 88-D-2.)

Figure 6. Old John Jumper, *niháɫákkohâ:ci*, Otter Clan, Mikasuki, Big Cypress family #13, and his family, with Will Stranahan at his brother Frank's trading post on the New River, before 1897. *Back row, right to left:* Billy Buck (?); Charley Willie (?); Will Stranahan; Frank Jumper (?). *Front row, right to left: hasati; lipáyki* (wife of Old John Jumper), Eufaula Clan, Creek Seminole; Old John Jumper; Ben Frank (boy kneeling). The two women on the left and the six small children (one barely discernible behind Ben Frank) are unidentified. Photograph by H. A. Ernst. (National Anthropological Archives, Smithsonian Institution, 1178-m-6-a.)

Figure 7. Four men, probably at Jupiter around 1879, photographed by M. E. Spencer. *Left:* Doctor's Boy; *right:* Little Tiger, *fakkilástihâ:ci*, Wildcat Clan, Mikasuki (Miami River family #21). *Standing with gun:* Robert Osceola, *katcamatâlki*, Panther Clan, Mikasuki (Miami River family #20). The second man from left is unidentified. Print from a glass stereopticon plate. (Historical Society of Palm Beach County, Peebles Collection, 42.)

Figure 8. Little Tiger, *fakkilástihâ:ci*, Wildcat Clan, Mikasuki, Miami River family #21 (see MacCauley, p. 507). His coat has an appliqué decoration, and he wears a woven beadwork sash, buckskin leggings, and new buckskin moccasins. According to MacCauley, Little Tiger, of the Wildcat Clan, was an exception to the standard matrilocal practice that a man moved to live with his wife and her family when they married. Little Tiger brought his wife, an Otter Clan member, to live with his Wildcat kin at the Miami River settlement. Print from a glass stereopticon plate, taken about 1879 by M. E. Spencer. (Historical Society of Palm Beach County, Peebles Collection, 41.)

Figure 9. Old Motlow, *hopa:yĩ:má:ɬi,* Wind Clan, Big Cypress family #5, at Coconut Grove about 1888. He wears a new set of Seminole-made clothes, with an appliqué design on his coat, a fine silver turban band, and buckskin leggings. Photograph by Ralph Middleton Munroe. (Historical Association of Southern Florida, 84D-2.)

Figure 10. Doctor Tiger, *abáyákhâ:ci*, Wildcat Clan, Mikasuki, younger brother of Little Tiger, Miami River family #21, about 1888, perhaps at Brickell's trading post on the Miami River. Photograph by Ralph Middleton Munroe. (Historical Association of Southern Florida, 169K.)

Figure 11. Cypress Charlie, *i:ma:łáhá:ci*, Panther Clan, Mikasuki, husband of *kasá:yi* (Fig. 5), Big Cypress family #12, about 1886 at Coconut Grove. Photograph by Ralph Middleton Munroe. (Historical Association of Southern Florida, 91D-2.)

Figure 12. Group of Seminole visitors in front of the Jupiter lighthouse in 1881. *Second from left:* Doctor's Boy; *boy seated at right:* perhaps Frank Tiger, *fö:shátki.* Print copied from a stereopticon glass plate taken by M. E. Spencer. (Historical Society of Palm Beach County, Peebles Collection, 48.)

Figure 13. Three men standing on a dock, Jupiter, 1879. *At left:* Doctor's Boy. Print copied from a stereopticon glass plate taken by M. E. Spencer. (Historical Society of Palm Beach County, Peebles Collection, 45.)

Figure 14. Group in front of the Jupiter lighthouse in 1879 or 1880. *Second from left:* Doctor's Boy. Print copied from a stereopticon glass plate taken by M. E. Spencer. (Historical Society of Palm Beach County, Peebles Collection, 46.)

Figure 15. Little Tiger, *fakkilástihâ:ci* (Wildcat Clan, Mikasuki, Miami River family #21), and party, about 1880, in a Seminole dugout canoe made with an adze borrowed from James A. Armoor, lighthouse keeper of Jupiter Light. Little Tiger is at far right, holding paddle. Copied from a stereopticon glass plate taken by M. E. Spencer. (Historical Society of Palm Beach County, Peebles Collection, 44.)

Figure 16. Doctor Tiger, *abáyákhâ:ci*, Wildcat Clan, Mikasuki, younger brother of Little Tiger, Miami River family #21, in a dugout canoe with mast for sailing, Miami River region, 1886. Photograph by Ralph Middleton Munroe. (Historical Association of Southern Florida, 150D.)

Figure 17. Five young Mikasuki men, all of the Otter Clan, dressed in largely non-Seminole clothes (very unusual for the period), 1892, Coconut Grove. Photograph by Ralph Middleton Munroe. *Back row, left to right:* Billy Doctor, *sō:nakyáhóli,* and Tommy Doctor, *i:kasháci,* both sons of Old Doctor, Miami River family #8; Charlie Cypress, *coko:thá:ci,* son of Cypress Charlie, Big Cypress family #12. *Front row, left:* Cuffney Tiger, *coko:thiníhi,* son of Little Tiger, Miami River family #21; *right,* Jackson Charley, *coko:tyáhóli.* Identifications by Charlie Cypress in 1952. (Historical Association of Southern Florida, 79D.)

Figure 18. Four young women standing beside the scoring marks on the goal post for the ball game at a Green Corn Dance at or near the Big Cypress settlement, between 1877 and 1892. Photograph by Charles Barney Cory. (National Anthropological Archives, Smithsonian Institution, WCS No. 6.18, Cory Collection.)

Figure 19. Lucy Gopher, *omalâyki*, Little Bird Clan, Creek Seminole, daughter of Martha Tiger and Old Tom Tiger, Cat Fish Lake family #34, on the way to the Big Cypress Green Corn Dance, between 1877 and 1892. Photograph by Charles Barney Cory. (National Anthropological Archives, Smithsonian Institution, 45,331-H.)

Figure 20. Tom Tiger, *míkkotástaná:ki*, Creek Seminole, with his daughter "Hi-e-tee," his wife "Ho-ti-yee," and his son Little Tiger, between 1877 and 1892. Tom Tiger evidently acquired this name after 1880 on the death of the previous *tástaná:ki* (both of them reported in Fish Eating Creek family #24). Photograph by Charles Barney Cory. (National Anthropological Archives, Smithsonian Institution, 45,491.)

MacCauley's 1880 Seminole Census

What follows is MacCauley's census of the Seminoles (as of October 1, 1880), taken from photostats of documents in Record Group 29 (1880 Census, Florida) in the National Archives. There, the five communities MacCauley censused are filed separately by county and given enumeration district numbers and page numbers. The family numbers assigned by MacCauley were retained, however; they indicate that he censused these communities in the following sequence, which matches the roman numerals he assigned to them on his map (p. 477). In order, the communities are:

I. The Big Cypress Swamp, Monroe County (Enumeration District No. 118, pp. 21–22; vol. 4, p. 293 and reverse of p. 293, micro T-9, roll 131). Families #1–14, enumerated in February 1881.

II. Miami River Settlement, Dade County (Enumeration District No. 25, pp. 5–6; vol. 1, p. 447, micro T-9, roll 126). Families #15–23, enumerated in February 1881.

III. Fish Eating Creek Settlement, Manatee County (Enumeration District No. 104, p. 74; vol. 4, p. 38, micro T-9, roll 130). Families #24–29, enumerated in February and March 1881.

IV. Cow Creek Settlement, Brevard County (Enumeration District No. 14, no page number; vol. 4, reverse of p. 38, micro T-9, roll 130). Families #30–32, enumerated in February and March 1881.

V. Cat Fish Lake Settlement, Polk County (Enumeration District No. 129, p. 66; vol. 5, p. 34, micro T-9, roll 131). Families #33–37, enumerated in March 1881.

In addition, a schedule was filled out in June 1880 by one J. Brady Brown, for 15 individuals in 3 Seminole families (#90–92) living "West of St Johns River, Brevard County" (Enumeration District No. 14, p. 13; vol. 1, reverse of p. 287, micro T-9, roll 126)—probably about 15 miles southwest of the present town of Melbourne. Brown's schedule gives only English individual names, whereas MacCauley's schedules give only Creek individual names. The relation of Brown's schedule to MacCauley's schedules is unclear. MacCauley's lists include 37 families and 208 individuals, which are the totals he gives on p. 477 of his report, where he also specifies "twenty-two camps," although camps are not indicated on his schedules.

MacCauley did not realize that there were (and still are) two distinct Indian languages spoken by the Florida Seminoles: Mikasuki and Creek. Most of the residents of the Big Cypress and Miami River regions were Mikasuki speakers, whereas most of those living in the other four areas were Creek speakers. The two languages are related but not mutually intelligible. There were probably more Mikasuki speakers who were also fluent in Creek than the reverse, and Creek had long been preferred for interaction with outsiders. This latter fact helps explain why Little Billie, MacCauley's guide and interpreter whose first language was Mikasuki, gave MacCauley individual names only as pronounced in Creek. Even among Mikasuki speakers, the Indian names of nearly all individuals were (and are) in Creek, although pronounced somewhat differently in a Mikasuki context.

Seminole Indian names are of two types: those of children and women, and those of adult men. Children's names are meaningful, and traditionally alluded to an experience (usually of the name-giver) during the Seminole wars. Such names are rarely given to more than one individual. Women kept (and still keep) their childhood names throughout their lives. However, boys were given a different name when they reached adulthood, and men sometimes received additional names to mark significant achievements. These men's names often cannot be fully translated by modern Seminoles, especially because they usually contain a word that is a title referring to a traditional Creek social status or politico-religious office, such as *há:co*, *i:ma:ɬá*, or *hinihá*. Most of these offices or statuses were lost when the Seminoles separated from the Creek Confederacy, but the titles survive in men's names.

In the listing below, the Indian names are first given in MacCauley's spellings as they appear on the census sheets. Below these, within square brackets, the names have been rewritten in the standard Creek spelling system by Lorene Gopher of the Brighton Reservation, whenever recognizable to her, during consultation in January 2000. These spellings are underlined. They are followed by phonemic spellings (in italics) of Creek, which I wrote, assisted by Sally McLendon, following the dictation of Lorene Gopher. For communities III–V, Happy Jones, Howard Micco, and Alice Snow, knowledgeable elders and speakers of Creek from the Brighton Reservation, were also consulted in January 2000, through the good offices of Tribal Chairman James E. Billie. Lorene Gopher provided En-

glish translations for the Creek names she recognized as such, and also
for names not known to her but recognizable as meaningful Creek words
from my trial pronunciations of MacCauley's spellings. Happy Jones,
Howard Micco, and Alice Snow confirmed these for names recognizable
to them from communities III–V.

In his report MacCauley gives a few of the English names of the people
he met and censused. In 1880, however, many Seminoles (especially
women) had not yet adopted English names. Most of the associations
with English names provided here come from my own work in the 1950s.
I did not know of the MacCauley census at that time, but I compiled
extensive genealogies from oral family traditions, and from showing old
photographs to knowledgeable elders. Especially important sources of
names (both Indian and English) and of genealogical relationships were
consultations with Josie Billie (*katcanokoftihá:ci*, Panther Clan), Charlie
Cypress (*coko:thá:ci*, Otter Clan), Ingram Billie (*nokakhá:ci*, Panther Clan),
William McKinley Osceola (*hinihákyaholí*, Town Clan), Billy Bowlegs
(*cofihâ:co*, Snake Clan), and Sam Huff (*hacikocókonihá:ci*, Town Clan).
Charlie Cypress and Billy Bowlegs were children when MacCauley carried out his census, and are included there (C.C., Big Cypress family #12;
B.B., Fish Eating Creek family #27). Sam Huff may have been born about
1880; his family is Miami River #19. Josie Billie and Ingram Billie were
the sons of Little Billie, MacCauley's most important teacher and con-
sultant, and his wife (Big Cypress family #14), and William McKinley
Osceola was the son of Robert Osceola, *katcamatalkí*, Panther clan (Miami River family #20, Fig. 7). They all thus grew up in these communities and knew the individuals MacCauley censused.

The printed forms provided to the census takers are arranged in columns to organize the information recorded about each individual.
MacCauley's handwritten entries are defined by the headings of these
columns, as follows (from left to right in each entry):

Families enumerated in order of visitation
The Name of each Person, whose place of abode, on 1ˢᵗ day of June,
    1880, was in this family
Color—White, W; Black, B; Mulatto, Mu; Chinese, C; Indian, I
Sex—Male, M; Female, F
Age at last birthday prior to June 1, 1880. If under 1 year, give months in
    fractions, thus: 3/12

Relationship of each person to the head of this family . . .

Single, Married, Widowed, Divorced

Profession, Occupation, or Trade . . . .

All the materials here added to MacCauley's recordings are placed within square brackets.

I. The Big Cypress Swamp

1 I-ful-lo-ha-tco; I; M; 35; Agriculture & Hunting &c.
[(as pronounced in Mikasuki) *ifolo:ha:cí*, Charley Osceola, Panther Clan. Owner of the first house seen by MacCauley, p. 499.]
_____; I; F; 27; wife; Agriculture & Housework
_____; I; F; 6/12; daughter

2 Tûs-ko-na; I; M; 24
[Tvskonv; *taskó:na*. MacCauley (p. 501) reports that this man's camp consisted of several families and possibly had a wet-weather kitchen.]
Ta-log-li´; I; F; 50; wife; Housework &c.
Pa-sak-ha-tco´; I; M; 18; stepson; single; Hunting & Herding
[(as pronounced in Mikasuki) *pahsákha:cí*, Jimmie Osceola, Panther Clan.]
Ko-la-ti-ha-tco; I; M; 16; stepson; single; Hunting & Herding
[(as pronounced in Mikasuki) *ko:lahtiha:cí*, Tommy Osceola, Panther Clan]
Hi´l-la-pai-i-ki; I; F; 14; stepdaughter; single; Home and field work
[Helvpake; *hilápâyki*, 'the one who does something fast,' Nancy Osceola, Panther Clan.]
Ätc-kis´-hā-tcō; I; M; 15; nephew; single; Hunting &c.
Sam-i´1-ho-i-yi´; I; F; 17; niece; single; Home & field work
[Semahoye; *sima:hóyi*, 'two people talking about something some where.']

3 Y´ul-ki-hā-tcō´; I; M; 20; Hunting & Agriculture
[*yolkihă:ci*, Tom Tiger, Town Clan.]
Fol-lai-ki; I; F; 20; wife; Housework & Agriculture
[Folike; *foléyki*, 'go back.']
_____; I; M; 1; child

4 Ka-tca-fiks-i-ko; I; M; 25; Hunting & Agriculture; pneumonia?

[Katcvfekseko; *katcafiksíko*, 'panther-(title),' Tony Tommie, Panther Clan.]

Pi´n-ka-lai-ki; I; F; ? (age); wife; Housework & Agriculture
[Penkvlike; *pinkaléyki*, 'the one who is afraid.']

_____; I; M; 3; son

_____; I; F; 3/12; child

Ya´-ho-la-ha´-tco; I; M; 36; brother-in-law; single; none (occupation); blind
[Yahulahaco; *yaholahá:co*, '(title)-(title).']

_____; I; F; 28; sister-in-law; single; Housework & Agriculture

I-tam-fi´ks-i-ko´; I; M; 16; ? (relationship); single; Hunting &c.

5 Ho-pai-yi-mac-la´; I; M; 47; Medicine man; Farming & Hunting
[Hopvye emarv; *hopayí i:ma:łá*, 'far away-(title),' Old Motlow, Wind Clan.]

Mai-yaq-ti´; I; F; 55; wife; Housework &c.
[Mayvtkv; *mayátka*, 'flaunting around.']

6 Tak´-o-si-mac-la´; I; M; 50; Agriculture & Hunting
[Tvkosemarv; *takosi:má:ła*, '(clan name)-(title),' Old Tommy—identified by MacCauley, who visited him and the Big Cypress group at his sugarcane field, pp. 501, 511.]

Na-sai-ki´; I; F; 60; wife; Agriculture & Housework

So-tsa-ha-tco´; I; M; 19; son; single; Agriculture &c.
[Sosvhaco; *só:sahá:co*, 'come out-(title).']

Nai-hi-ya´; I; M; 17; son; single; Agriculture &c.

Tco-fo-lop-hā´-tco´; I; M; 16; son; single; Agriculture &c.
[Cofoluthaco; '*cofolóthá:co*, 'turn deer-(title)'; or in Mikasuki '*cofolopha:cí*, Little Charlie Jumper, Panther Clan.]

Toq-ki; I; M; 14; son; single; Agriculture &c.

7 Tal-ki-ha-tco; I; M; 35; Agriculture & Hunting
[Hotvlkehaco; *hotalkihá:co*, Key West Billy (Billy Fewell), Wind Clan—described as "progressive" by MacCauley, pp. 484–485, 501, and pictured by MacCauley on p. 484 and in Figs. 1 and 2 in this introduction. MacCauley did not hear the initial syllable of his name.]

I-hai-ki; I; F; 30; wife; Agriculture & Housework
[Ehvlke, from Mikasuki *ihálki*, '(someone's) wife.']

Tca-kai-i-ki; I; M; 12; son

_____; I; F; 4; daughter

_____; I; M; 9/12; child

8 Ho-töl-gi-a-ho-la´; I; M; 40; Medicine man

[Hotvlkeyaholv; *hotálki yahóla*, 'wind-(title),' Old Doctor, Wind Clan.]

Ak-his-ho-i-yi´; I; F; 40; wife; Agriculture &c.

[Vkkeshoye; *akkisho:yí*, 'they picked her up from a low place' (e.g., from water).]

Tsa-tiq-tsi´; I; F; 16; daughter; single; Agriculture & Housework

Si´m-mi-si´; I; M; 13; son; Hunting &c.

[Semese; *simi:sí*, 'to take something from someone (to help them).']

Sim-mai-yi-pi´; I; F; 12; daughter; Housework &c.

[Semvyehpe; *simayihpí*, 'to take something from someone and go with it.']

I-tsai-hi; I; M; 11; son; Hunting &c.

[Ecvhe; from Mikasuki *icá:hi*, 'older brother.']

I-clan-i-la´ki´; I; M; 10; son; Hunting &c.

_____; I; F; daughter

Clak-ma-ti´; I; F; 60; mother-in-law; divorced

[Perhaps Rakkvte; *łakka:tí*, 'the big one.']

_____; I; F; 45; ? (relationship); widowed/divorced

9 Hâl-pa-ta´-hā-tcō; I; M; 35; Agriculture & Hunting

[Hvlpvtvhaco; *halpatahá:co*, 'alligator-(title).']

Pin-no-ti´; I; F; 29; wife; Agriculture & Housework

[Perhaps Penute; *pino:tí*, 'our teeth.']

Clas-li´b-ai-ki; I; M; 13; son; Hunting &c.

Tco-ko-la-ki´; I; M; 10; son

[Cukolike; *cokolêyki*, 'someone who's home all the time / where the house sits.']

Ka-pis´-lai-tsi´; I; F; 4; daughter

[Kvpeslicet; *kapísleycit*, 'she always has lye.']

10 Ko-nip´-i-ya-ho-la´; I; M; 35; Agriculture & Hunting

[(as pronounced in Mikasuki) *konipyaholí*, Miami Billy, Wind Clan.]

Ak-lo-pi´; I; F; 27; wife; Agriculture & Housework

[<u>Vklope</u>; *aklopí*, 'the one taking a bath, bathing.']
Il-lan-wí'; I; M; 11; son; Hunting &c.
   [<u>Elawe</u>; *iláwi*, 'hungry.']
_____; I; F; 10; daughter
_____; I; F; 9; daughter
_____; I; F; 4; daughter

11 Tûs-ta-na-ka-ha-tco; I; M; 87; Medicine man
   [<u>Tvstvnvkehaco</u>; *tastanakiháco*, '(title)-(title),' probably Billy Harney,
   Otter Clan.]
_____; I; F; ? (age); wife; Housework &c.
Is-wûl-ki; I; F; 12; daughter
Ko-mai-ki; B; F; 30; ? (relationship); single; Housework &c. Adopted into
   the tribe when young.
   [*komâyki* (meaning?)]
Ho-tal-i'; I ½ ; M; 10; ? (relationship)
   [<u>Hotvle</u>; *hotalí*, 'wind.']

12 I-mac-li-ha-tco; I; M; 30; Agriculture & Hunting
   [<u>Emarvhaco</u>; *i:ma:ɫahá:co*, '(title)-(title),' Cypress Charley, Panther
   Clan; see Fig. 11.]
Ka-sai-yi; I; F; 27; wife; Agriculture & Housework
   [Perhaps *kashá:yi*, 'a kind of berry'; in Mikasuki *kasá:yi*; see Fig. 5.]
_____; I; M; 10; son
_____; I; M; 7; son
_____; I; F; 3; daughter

13 I-ya-ho-li'-mac-la'; I; M; 40; Medicine man
   [<u>Eyvholemarv</u>; *i:yaholi:má:ɫa*, '(title)-(title).']
_____; I; F; 35; wife; Agriculture & Housework
Sit'-a-piks-i-ha-tco; I; M; 18; son; single; Hunting &c.
   [<u>Tvpeksehaco</u>; *tapiksihá:co*, 'bear paws-(title),' or perhaps *ciktopik-*
   sihá:co, 'king snake-(title).']
No-ko-si-ha'-tco; I; M; 17; son; single; Hunting &c.
   [<u>Nokosehaco</u>; *nokosihá:co*, 'bear-(title).']
_____; I; M; 10; son

Ni-hac-lak´-ut-tsi´; I; M; 90; ? (relationship); widowed/divorced; Medicine man; Deaf and blind from old age
[Neharakkoce; nihaɫakko:cí, 'little big fat,' or perhaps nihalakkohá:ci, 'big fat-(title),' Old Jumper, Otter Clan; see Fig. 6.]

14 Fo-si-mac-la´; I; M; 40; Agriculture & Hunting
[Fusemarv; fosi:má:ɫa, 'bird-(title).']
Aq-ti´; I; F; 40; wife; Agriculture & Housework
Ko-nip-ha-tco; I; M; 22; single; Herding & Hunting; Attended school within the Census year; Reads and writes a very little
[Konvphaco; ko:naphá:co (in Mikasuki konipha:cí), '(meaning?)-(title),' Little Billy, Billy Conepatchie, Wind Clan—MacCauley's main guide and interpreter (see pp. 492–494).]

II. Miami River Settlement

15 Tco-kot-i-mac-la´; I; M; 40; Medicine man
[Cukotemarv; coko:ti:ma:ɫá, 'house-(title),' Young Tigertail, husband of Mo-ki—according to MacCauley (p. 488).]
Mo-ki´; I; F; 29; wife; Agriculture & Housework
[Mokke; mokkí, 'smoke.']
A-nak-ti´; I; M; 4; son
_____; I; F; 1; daughter; sick, swollen leg
A-ho-i´;I; F; 40; wife; Agriculture &c.
[Ahoye; a:ho:yí, 'two people going.']
Pa-lo-hai-ki´; I; F; 17; daughter; single; Housework &c.
[(as pronounced in Mikasuki) palohâyki (meaning?).]
Ta-nit-tsai´-tsi; I; F; 8; daughter
[Tvnecice; taníceycí, 'the one that empties out.']
_____; I; F; 7
Tcat-tsi; I; M; 4; son
[ca:cí, 'I want.']

16 Hin-ni-ya-ho-li´; I; M; 43; married; Jeweler, Hunter, &c.; Medicine man
[hiniyaho:lí 'road' (in Mikasuki)-'(title),' Old Tommy, takosa:ɫí Clan.]
_____; I; F; 38; wife; Housework &c.

Ko-tcak´-a-na-ha-tco; I; M; 20; son; single; Agriculture & Hunting
[Kocuknehaco; *kocokniháːco*, 'short one-(title).']
Ha-clan-ha-tco; I; M; 19; son; single; Agriculture & Hunting
[(as pronounced in Mikasuki) *hałanhaːcí*, Big Tommy, Bird Clan.]
Ta-mi-ha-tco; I; M; 17; son; single; Agriculture & Hunting
[(as pronounced in Mikasuki) *tamihaːcí*, Doctor Tommy, Bird Clan.]
Si-ka-pa-ki; F; 14; daughter; single
[Sekvpake; *siːkapâːki*, 'the one who separates from their group.']
_____; I; F; 12; daughter

17 Ho-nis-ha-tco´; I; M; 38; Agriculture & Hunting
[(as pronounced in Mikasuki) *hoːnishaːcí*, Cypress Tiger, Otter Clan.]
Tsi-ca-yi; I; F; 38; wife; Agriculture & Housework
[Resiye; *łisaːyí*, 'they're going.']
Tai-yi-tsai´-tsi; I; M; 13; son; Hunting, &c.
Hûm´-ki; I; F; 18; stepdaughter; single; Housework &c.
[*hámki*, 'one' (doubtful as a name).]
_____; I; M; 11; son by a former wife
Mi-ful-lai-ki; I; F; 19; stepdaughter and wife; Housework &c.
[Mvfolike; *máfolêyki*, 'the one who went back to them/her.']
_____; I; M; 14; son; single
_____; I; M; 2; son
Pa-lul-li´; I; F; 55; ? (relationship); widowed/divorced; Agriculture &c.

18 0-tsis-si´; I; M; 44; Agriculture & Hunting
[*ocísi*, '(band name, in Oklahoma Creek),' Old Doctor, Bird (?) Clan.]
I-ham-ho-ki; I; F; 30; wife; Agriculture & Housework;
[Ehvmhoke; *iːhamhôːki*, 'being brave.']
It´-ko-ho-li´; I; M; 8; son
_____; I; F; 6; daughter

19 Bûf´-fût-ha-tco; I; M; 38; Agriculture & Hunting
[Old Charlie (Huff?); Lorene Gopher suggested the first part of the name
could be a form of the verb *póːfkit*, 'to blow'; the last part is *háːco*,
'(title).']
Ma-ha-yäk´-tsi; I; F; 30; wife; Agriculture & Housework
No-kiq-tsi; I; M; 11; son
_____; I; F; 6; daughter

Sa-ho-yi-i-cli; I; F; 23; wife; Agriculture & Housework
    [Svhoyehere; *sahoyihíłi,* 'their (dual) way (of life) is good.']
    _____; I; M; 4; son
So-lot-ho´-ki or So-ho-lot-ki; I; F; 60; mother-in-law; widowed/divorced;
    Agriculture & Housework
    [Soluthoke; *solothô:ki,* 'lying on ground creeping.']
Ko-ti-ha-tco; I; M; 16; brother-in-law; single; Hunting &c.
    [Kutehaco; *kotihá:co,* 'frog-(title),' (Old) Charlie Willie, Town Clan.]

20 Kā-tca-ma´-tûl-ka´; I; M; 25; Agriculture & Hunting
    [Katcvmatvlkv; *ka:tcamatâlki,* 'panther-the only one,' Robert Osceola,
    Panther Clan.]
Nı́l-la´-ki´; I; F; 17; wife; Agriculture & Housework
    _____; I; M; 3/12 Summer; child

21 Fûk-i-lûs-ti´; I; M; 35; Agriculture & Hunting
    [Fvkkelvste; *fakkilásti,* 'black clay,' Little Tiger, Wildcat Clan. MacCauley
    mentions him (p. 507) as "a rather important personage" whose Otter
    Clan wife moved to his camp, contrary to the usual matrilocal pattern;
    see Figs. 7, 8, 15.]
Bit´-tci´; I; F; 29; wife; Agriculture & Housework
Yo-pa-ha-ki´;I; M; 12; son; Hunting &c.
    [Yupvhake; *yopahá:ki,* 'falling behind (a group).']
Kop-ti-ni´ ? ; I; M; 10; son
    _____; I; M; 8; son
    _____; I; F; 3; child
Kaq-pi; I; F; 60; mother; widowed/divorced; Agriculture &c.
    [Kvpe; *kapí,* 'lye.']
Fis-taq-ki´; I; F; 35; sister; single; Agriculture & Housework
A´-ba-yik´-ha-tco; I; M; 19; brother; single; Hunting &c.
    [Apeyvkhaco; *apiyakhá:co* (Mikasuki *abáyákhâ:ci*), 'people going-
    (title),' Doctor Tiger,Wildcat Clan; see Figs. 10, 16.]
Hi-tcai´-ki; I; F; 58; mother-in-law; widowed/divorced; Agriculture &c.
    [Hecvke; *hica:kí,* 'they see.']
Hin-ni-ha-mik´-ko; I; M; 90; ? (relationship); widowed/divorced
    [Henehamekko; *hiniha:míkko,* '(title)-(title).']
To-koc-lai´-ki; I; F; 19; ? (relationship); single; Housework

[Tokorike; *tokołêyki*, 'two people running.']

Ka-tsa-ha-tco; M; I; 17; ? (relationship); single; Hunting &c
[Katcvhaco, *kátcahâ:co*, 'panther-(title).']

Ya-ta-wa-ha-tco´ ; M; I; 15; ? (relationship); single; Hunting &c.
[Yatvwvhaco; *ya:tawahâ:co*, 'in this place-(title).']

22 Ya-ha-ha-tco; I; M; 26; Agriculture & Hunting
[Yvhahaco; *yahahá:co*, 'wolf-(title),' Little Billie Jim, Bear Clan.]

Ko-clip´-i´; I; F; 25; wife; Agriculture & Housework

_____; I; M; 2; son

23 Ni-hac-lak´-i-mac-la´; I; M; 40; Agriculture & Hunting &c.
[Neharakemarv; *ni:ha:łáki:má:ła*, 'big fat-(title).']

Sa-na-hi´-to-i; I; F; 32; wife; Agriculture & Housework

Ko-wa´-kûts-la-ni´; I; M; 19; son; single; Hunting &c.
[Kowakkotslane; *kowa:kóclâ:ni*, 'yellow wildcat.']

Ha-sa-tiq´-tsi; I; F; 10; daughter
[Hasvtece; *hasatíci*, 'cleaning, the one that cleans.']

_____; I; M; 6; son

_____; I; F; 5; daughter

III. Fish Eating Creek Settlement

24 Tûs-tä-nûg-g´e; I; M; 80; Chief of tribes, medicine man, Agriculture &
Hunting
[Tvstvnvke; *míkkotástanáki* (also simply *tástanáki*), 'chief-(title).' "The
old chief" who refused to cooperate with MacCauley (p. 491).]

Hos-pa-ta-ki´; I; M; 78; brother; widowed/divorced; Medicine man, Agriculture and Hunting
[Hospvtake; *hospata:kí* (meaning?).]

Ka-tca-la-ni; I; M; 33; ? (relationship); widowed/divorced; Agriculture &
Hunting
[Katcvlane; *katcalá:ni*, 'yellow panther,' Capt. Tom Tiger, Panther Clan.
MacCauley mentions hunting with him (pp. 492, 512), and how he dem-
onstrated lighting a fire with flint and steel, p. 518; probably in Fig. 20.]

_____; I; F; 60; Ka-tca-la-ni's mother; widowed/divorced; Agricul-
ture & Housework

25 Ho-laq'-to-mik'ko ; I; M; 70; Agriculture, Hunting &c.
[Holattvmekko; *holáttamí:kko*, 'blue/green chief'; the first element was recorded in the 1950s as *holáhta*, a title, whereas H. J., H. M., and A. S. suggested *folápa* or *falápa*, 'shell.']

A-nai-tci ; I; F; 65?; wife; Agriculture & Housework
[Anihce; *a:nêyhci*, 'helping, the one who helps'; L. G. suggested it could also be *a:níhci*.]

Tca-yai-yak-tsi; I; F; 20; daughter; single; Agriculture & Housework
[perhaps *cayayyákit*, 'hush, be quiet.']

It-tcai-hi; I; M; 16; son; single; Hunting &c.
[Etciye; *ítcâyi*, 'shooting, the one who shoots.']

Is-ti-ma-pa-ka; I; M; 11; son
[Estemapakv; *istimapâ:ki*, 'person joining a group.']

26 Ak-fûs-ki'; I; M; 35; Agriculture & Hunting
[Vkfvske; *akfáski*, 'toward a point,' Tommy Micco, Otter Clan.]

Tcan-ho'-ka; I; F; 26; wife; Agriculture & Housework
[Acvnhokv; *acanhô:ka* (shortened to '*canhô:ka*) 'it's already poured in.']

Ho-po'-clin-ai-ke'; I; F; 6; daughter
[Hoporenike; *hopoɬinêyki*, 'the one that's wise.']

Mi't-tai'-ki; I; F; ? (age); daughter
[Metetvkke; *mititáhki*, 'get ready.']

Ma-ho'-hi-yi; I; F; 45; mother-in-law; widowed/divorced; Agriculture & Housework

Kâi-yo-hoq'-ki; I; F; 25; sister-in-law; single; Agriculture & Housework
[Kâi-yo unrecognized; hoq'-ki perhaps **Hokte**; *hoktí*, 'female, woman.']

Ho-ma-hai'-ti; I; M; 16; brother-in-law; single; Hunting &c.
[Homv vyvte; *homa á:yiti*, 'he went in front, the leader.']

Pa-lat'-ka ; I; F; 7; sister-in-law
[Palatkv; *pa:lá:tka*, '(water) spilling.']

27 Osän/Ocän-a-ha-tco; I; M; 80; Agriculture &c.
[Osvnnvhaco; *osannahá:co*, 'otter-(title).']

Poq-ti; B; F; 75; wife; Agriculture &c.; Black adopted into the tribe
[Perhaps *pókta*, 'twin,' although this seems inappropriate as a name.]

Tsí't-to-lûs´-ti´; I ½; M; 23; son; single; Agriculture & Hunting
[Cektolvste; *cíktolásti*, 'black snake.']

Is-ti-mai-tca-ka ; I ½; F; 30; daughter; divorced; Agriculture & Housework
[Estemencvkv; *istimincá:ka*, 'stingy person'; or perhaps *istimacá:ka*, 'saved person'; probably Old Nancy, mother of *cofihá:co*, Billy Bowlegs.]

Tco-fi-ha-tco; I ½; M; 14; single
[Cufehaco; *cofihá:co*, 'rabbit-(title)'; Billy Bowlegs, Snake Clan.]

_____; I ½ ; M; 14; single

28   Tsit-to-ha-tco; I; M; 37; Agriculture & Hunting
[Cektohaco; *cíktohá:co*, 'snake-(title).']

Pai-i-hu-tci; I; F; 35? (age); wife; Agriculture & Housework
[Pvheoce; *paho:cí*, 'small grass' or 'where grass is' or 'she has grass.']

Cla-cu-la-te-ki; I; F; 35; sister-in-law; single; chronic rheumatism
[Rasulvtake; *ɬa:solatêyki*, 'it fell back on her,' or possibly *ɬakalatéyki*, 'fell down.']

29   Ak-ta-ya-ci-ha´-tco; I; M; 23; single; Agriculture & Hunting

Ci-ha´-ne; I; F; 60; mother; widowed/divorced; Agriculture & Housework
[Sehane; *síha:ní*, 'someone gets mad at you'; older pronunciation *ciha:ní*.]

Pal-pa-ki; I; F; 30; sister; single; Agriculture & Housework
[Pvlpake; *palpâ:ki*, 'roll, roll over.']

Tai-ko-tci; I; F; 22; sister; single; Agriculture & Housework
[Tikoci; *tayko:cí* (in Mikasuki, 'girl, little woman').]

Ki-ho-hi-yi; I; F; 15; sister; single; Agriculture & Housework

Ho-la-ta-ha-tco; I; M; 16; brother; single; Hunting &c.

[Holattvhaco; *holáttahá:co*, 'blue/green-(title)'; or perhaps *foláhtahá:co*, the name of George Billie, who died in 1935. Cf. Ho-laq-to-mik-ko, under family #25 above.]

IV. Cow Creek Settlement

30   Hin-hi-mac-la´; I; M; 45; Agriculture, Hunting &c.
[Henehemarv; *hinihi:ma:ɬá*, '(meaning?)-(title).']

Mis-sit-ho´-i-yi; I; F; 45; wife; Agriculture & Housework
[Mesethoye; *misithó:yih*, '(several) blinking their eyes.']

Fus-ha-tco´; I; M; 27; ? (relationship); single; Medicine man; Agriculture & Hunting
[Fushaco; *foshá:co,* 'bird-(title).']
Yo-pak-i-lät´-ke; I; F; 17; ? (relationship); single; Agriculture & Housework
[Yupvvklvtke; *yópa aklátki,* 'it fell behind (something).']
A-si-ho´-ki; I; M; 13; ? (relationship); Hunting &c.
[Asehoke; *a:sihô:ki,* 'they've gotten up, they're standing there.']

31 Ko-wa´-kats-ha-tco; I; M; 29; Medicine man; Agriculture & Hunting
[Kowakkotshaco; *kowa:kóchâ:co,* 'wildcat-(title).']
Ma-ti-lûk-ki´; I; F; 28; wife; Agriculture & Housework
_____; I; ? (sex); ? (age); child

32 Ta-la-ma-si´; I; M; 25; Agriculture, Hunting, &c.
[*ta:la:má:hi,* perhaps 'where the swamp cabbage grows' (not a man's name); or *talimá:si* (perhaps a Mikasuki word), 'something used to be there.']
Na-ta-si´; I; F; 21; wife; Agriculture and Housework
[Natakse; *natáksi,* 'raising one's chin.']
A-fa-na-ka´; I; M; 3; son
[Affvnnvkv; *affánnaka,* 'a lookout (person).']
_____; I; M; 2; son

V. Cat Fish Lake Settlement

33 (It)Tco-i-mac-la-tcûp-ko; I; M; 90; Agriculture & Housework
[Coemaracvpko; *'co i:mɑ:lacápko,* 'deer-(title)-long,' (Old) Chipco or Tcup-ko—mentioned by MacCauley on p. 504.]
Los-ta´; I; F; 65; wife; Agriculture & Housework

34 Ko-i-ha-tco; I; M; 35; Hunting & Agriculture
[Kowehaco; *ko:wihá:co,* 'wildcat' (in Mikasuki)-'(title),' Big (or Old) Tom Tiger, Panther Clan.]
Tai-has-tci; I; F; 30; wife; Housework & Agriculture
[Martha Tiger, Little Bird Clan; see Fig. 4.]
Tin´-fai-yai-ki; I; M; 12; son; Hunting &c.
[Tenfayake; *tinfaya:kí,* 'uneven edges'—mentioned by MacCauley, p. 482. Probably Tommy John, Little Bird Clan.]

O-mäl-lai-ki; I; F; 8; daughter; Housework
[Omalike; *omalêyki*, 'all of them'; later married Billy Stewart (Fig. 4).]
Täl-la-has-so-wi; I; F; 10; Housework
Cin´-wai-ho-yi; I; F; 6; daughter
[Cenwihoy; *cinwéyhó:yí*, 'they sold you something,' or *cinwéyhó:kí*, 'they've given it to you,' Emma Osceola; see Fig.4.]
Cla-sin´-to-ko-clai-ki; I; F; 4; daughter
[Rasentokorrike; *ła:sintokołêyki*, 'two of us ran from you (carrying something).']
Ce-ke-ka; I; F; 17; ? (relationship); Housework

35 Fue-tûs-ta-nûg-ge; I; M; 45; widowed/divorced; Hunting & Agriculture
[Fustvstvnvke; *fostastanáki*, 'bird-(title),' Tallahassee, Little Bird Clan— mentioned by MacCauley (p. 492) as taking care of his small child after his wife had recently died (p. 526); see Fig. 4.]
Mo-tsu-mai-ki´; I; M; 18; son; single; Hunting & Agriculture
[Mvksumike; *maksomêyki*, 'go under the water,' Billy Buster, Deer Clan.]
So-ho-lit-ka; I; M; 16; son; single; Hunting & Agriculture
[Soholetkv; *soholítka*, 'run (plurally) to something or somebody (if in trouble),' Billy Ham, Deer Clan.]
Sa-si-tci; I; M; 14; son; single; Hunting & Agriculture
[Svhece; *sahî:ci*, 'looking really straight ahead,' Young Tallahassee or Taklahassee-Chipco, Deer Clan.]
Fäl-le-nai´-ki; I; M; 10; son
[Fvlenake; *falinêyki*, 'dodger, dodging, flanking,' Mister Dennis, Deer Clan.]
Cuq´fa-nai´-ki; I; M; 8; son
[Cuffvnike; *coffanêyki*, 'taller than you, stand above you,' Deer Clan.]
Ya-wi-lai-yi; I; M; 6; son
[Tommy Hill, died about 1886–1888, Deer Clan; see Fig. 4. His age may be wrong here, for MacCauley says that Tallahassee's sons ranged in age from four to eighteen years, and describes him as a baby boy (p. 491).]

36 It-tcu-ha-tcu-si´; I; M; 35; Agriculture & Hunting
[Ecohacuce; *icoha:có:ci*, 'deer-(title)-little,' probably Deer Clan.]

Pa-caq´-ki; I; F; 45; wife; Agriculture & Housework
  [Pasake; *pasâ:ki*, 'brushing, rubbing,' or *pasákki*, 'to kill' (though this
  seems inappropriate as a name).]
Hä-na-sa; I; F; 25; wife; Agriculture & Housework
  [Perhaps Yamasv; *yamása*, 'tame.']
It-tcu´-il-li-ha´-tcu; I; M; ? 6 (age); son
  [Ecoelehaco; *icóiliháco*, 'deer foot-(title).']
I-tcok´-a-na-hi´; I; M; ?4 (age); son
  [Ecuknahv; *icokná:ha*, 'talking a lot.']
Cin´-naq-ki´; I; M; ? (age); son
  [Cenake; *cinâ:ki*, 'yours.']
Pi´f-fát-ka; I; M; ? (age); son
  [Pefvtkv; *pifátka*, '(more than one) running.']
_____; I; F; Baby 3/12; daughter

37 Si-si; B; F; 45; single; House-work & Agriculture; Adopted into the
  tribe when a child.
  [Sese; *sî:si*, 'carry,' or perhaps the English name "Sissy."]
Han-ne; B; F; 20; daughter; Housework & Agriculture
  [Perhaps Vne; *aní*, 'I, me,' although this seems unsuitable as a name;
  or perhaps the English name "Hannah."]
Me-le; I ½; M; 23; son; Hunting & Agriculture
  [Perhaps Amele; *a:mílli*, 'pointing,' John Willis Micco, described by
  MacCauley on p. 490.]

West of St. Johns River, Brevard County

(Enumerated by J. Brady Brown)
90 Parker, Streety; I; M; 60; Sub Chief
_____, Mrs.; I; F; 50; wife; Granddaughter of Billy Bow Legs
_____, Tom; I; M; 22; son; single; Warrior
_____, Miss; I; F; 12; daughter; At Home
_____, Henry; I; M; 10; son; At Home
_____, Miss; I; F; 7; daughter; At Home
91 Smith, Billy; I; M; 27; Warrior
_____, Olive; I; F; 18; wife; Keeping House
_____, Miss; I; F; 3; daughter; At Home
_____, Boy; I; M; 2; son; At Home

_____, Pickaniny; I; M; 2/12; son; At Home

92 Billy Sam; I; M; 22; Warrior

_____, Mrs.; I; F; 16; wife; Keeping House

_____, Boy; I; M; 2; son; At Home

_____, Miss; I; F; 1; daughter; At Home

J. W. POWELL'S INTRODUCTION
TO MACCAULEY'S
"THE SEMINOLE INDIANS OF FLORIDA"

The Indians known as Seminole are of the Muskokian linguistic stock who before the present century left their congeners and dwelt within the present limits of Georgia and Florida. A chief cause of the separation was disagreement among the people of the towns of the Lower Creeks and Hichiti concerning their relations with Europeans settling in the country. It is asserted that many turbulent and criminal Indians joined the emigrants, and thus the word "Seminole" or "Simanólë"—meaning separatist or renegade—became a term of opprobrium applied by the Creeks who had remained in their ancient seats. It is however to be noted that the present inhabitants of the Everglades repudiate the title and cast it back upon the much larger portion of their people now in the Indian Territory, thus impugning their courage and steadfastness, probably in allusion to the fact that the latter succumbed to the power of the United States in their deportation. The Apalachi, Timucua, and others of the earliest known inhabitants of the Floridian peninsula had been driven away and nearly exterminated in the wars of 1702 to 1708, leaving an immense tract of territory vacant for the Seminole migration, and some of the Muskoki were established in the southernmost part of the peninsula at the middle of the sixteenth century. Probably the people who are the subject of this paper are in part their descendants, while others may be descended from comers of a century later, but they are probably all the offspring of the determined band who, though defeated in war, would never submit to the Government of the United States, but retreated to the inaccessible cypress swamps, while the majority of their surviving comrades removed to the Indian Territory, another body having fled into Mexico. The Seminole war of 1835 to 1842 was the most stubbornly contested of all the Indian wars, and, considering the numerical force of the tribe, or perhaps even without that qualification, was the most costly and disastrous to the United States. During the seven years mentioned nearly every regiment of the regular army was engaged against them, besides marines and sailors, and in addition, for longer or shorter periods, 50,000 militia and volunteers. The cost of the war was $30,000,000 and over 3,000 lives. Of the Seminole probably not more than 400 warriors were engaged, their numerical weakness being counterbalanced by the topographic character of the country which they defended.

The Seminole, who are described in the present paper as of a high grade in physique and intelligence, may well be descendants of these heroes. It was natural that their inherited enmity and also their sense of danger should have induced them during the last half century to repel all visits from whites, and more especially from representatives of the United States Government. Their dwellings and villages have been so located as to secure this isolation, and the account now given of them by the Rev. Clay MacCauley, D. D., is the result of the first successful attempt to ascertain their true numbers and condition. Notwithstanding his ingenuity and energy, the adverse circumstances did not permit this investigation to be exhaustive; but it has been sufficient to discover some important and instructive facts set forth in the present essay.

The status of these Indians is peculiar in that their contact with civilization has hitherto been regulated, to an extent not known elsewhere, by their own volition, and has not been imposed upon them. Visitors, traders, and Government agents have been denied admission, but the Indians have in a limited way visited the settlements beyond their own boundaries and traded there. The result has been a remarkable prosperous condition in agriculture and domestic industries. This is not to be attributed wholly to the favorable character of their soil and climate, as under similar environment many peoples are lazy and improvident, whereas the Seminole of Florida are industrious and frugal. That they have advanced in culture during the last generation is doubtless true, but it is a common and pernicious error to consider the Indian tribes at the time of the Columbian discovery as wholly without knowledge of agriculture, depending solely on the chase, fishing, and the spontaneous products of the earth. This error is a part of the faræ naturæ theory which has been so baneful in the past consideration of the aboriginal inhabitants. No radical change was necessary for the greater portion of the Indian tribes to become self supporting by the industries classed as civilized, provided that their treatment had been rational and in accordance with the slow but certain operations of nature. Throughout the continent generally the pressure of the white settlers did not allow of the necessary delay, but here it was obtained. The advance of the Seminole has been practically without European instruction, the efforts of the Spanish missionaries of the seventeenth century having only left some traces of interpolation in their myths. They have adopted from European civilization some weapons, implements, and fabrics and have shown their capacity for imitation and adaptation; but their progress toward civilization has been their own work in the orderly course of evolution, and is therefore instructive.

SEMINOLE INDIANS OF FLORIDA

by Clay MacCauley

Letter of Transmittal

Minneapolis, Minn., June 24, 1884.

Sir: During the winter of 1880-81 I visited Florida, commissioned by you to inquire into the condition and to ascertain the number of the Indians commonly known as the Seminole then in that State. I spent part of the months of January, February, and March in an endeavor to accomplish this purpose. I have the honor to embody the result of my work in the following report.

On account of causes beyond my control the paper does not treat of these Indians as fully as I had intended it should. Owing to the ignorance prevailing even in Florida of the locations of the homes of the Seminole and also to the absence of routes of travel in Southern Florida, much of my time at first was consumed in reaching the Indian country. On arriving there, I found myself obliged to go among the Indians ignorant of their language and without an interpreter able to secure me intelligible interviews with them except in respect to the commonest things. I was compelled, therefore, to rely upon observation and upon very simple, perhaps misunderstood, speech for what I have here placed on record. But while the report is only a sketch of a subject that would well reward thorough study, it may be found to possess value as a record of facts concerning this little-known remnant of a once powerful people.

I have secured, I think, a correct census of the Florida Seminole by name, sex, age, gens, and place of living. I have endeavored to present a faithful portraiture of their appearance and personal characteristics, and have enlarged upon their manners and customs, as individuals and as a society, as much as the material at my command will allow; but under the disadvantageous circumstances to which allusion has already been made, I have been able to gain little more than a superficial and partial knowledge of their social organization, of the elaboration among them of the system of gentes, of their forms and methods of government, of their tribal traditions and modes of thinking, of their religious beliefs and practices, and of many other things manifesting what is distinctive in the life of a people. For these reasons I submit this report more as a guide for future investigation than as a completed result.

At the beginning of my visit I found but one Seminole with whom I could hold even the semblance of an English conversation. To him I am indebted for a large part of the material here collected. To him, in particular, I owe the extensive Seminole vocabulary now in possession of the Bureau of Ethnology. The knowledge of the Seminole language which I gradually acquired enabled me, in my intercourse with other Indians, to verify and increase the information I had received from him.

In conclusion, I hope that, notwithstanding the unfortunate delays which have occurred in the publication of this report, it will still be found to add something to our knowledge of this Indian tribe not without value to those who make their peculiar study.

Very respectfully,

CLAY MacCAULEY

MAJ. J. W. POWELL,
Director, Bureau of Ethnology

Introduction

There were in Florida, October 1, 1880, of the Indians commonly known as Seminole, two hundred and eight. They constituted thirty-seven families, living in twenty-two camps, which were gathered into

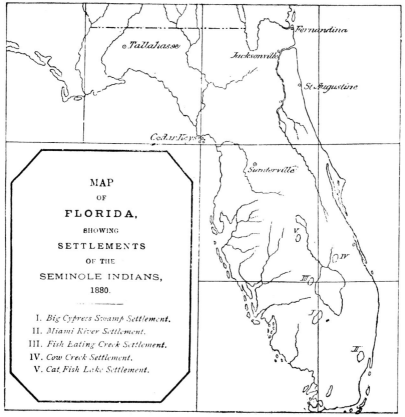

MAP

OF

FLORIDA,

SHOWING

SETTLEMENTS

OF THE

SEMINOLE INDIANS,

1880.

I. *Big Cypress Swamp Settlement.*
II. *Miami River Settlement.*
III. *Fish Eating Creek Settlement.*
IV. *Cow Creek Settlement.*
V. *Cat Fish Lake Settlement.*

FIG. 60. Map of Florida.

five widely separated groups or settlements. These settlements, from the most prominent natural features connected with them, I have named,

(1) The Big Cypress Swamp settlement; (2) Miami River settlement; (3) Fish Eating Creek settlement; (4) Cow Creek settlement; and (5) Cat Fish Lake settlement. Their locations are, severally: The first, in Monroe County, in what is called the "Devil's Garden," on the northwestern edge of the Big Cypress Swamp, from fifteen to twenty miles southwest of Lake Okeechobee; the second, in Dade County, on the Little Miami River, not far from Biscayne Bay, and about ten miles north of the site of what was, during the great Seminole war, Fort Dallas; the third, in Manatee County, on a creek which empties from the west into Lake Okeechobee, probably five miles from its mouth; the fourth, in Brevard County, on a stream running southward, at a point about fifteen miles northeast of the entrance of the Kissimmee River into Lake Okeechobee; and the fifth, on a small lake in Polk County, lying nearly midway between lakes Pierce and Rosalie, towards the headwaters of the Kissimmee River. The settlements are from forty to seventy miles apart, in an otherwise almost uninhabited region, which is in area about sixty by one hundred and eighty miles. The camps of which each settlement is composed lie at distances from one another varying from a half mile to two or more miles. In tabular form the population of the settlements appears as follows:

Settlements	Camps.	Population.													
		Divided according to age and sex.												Résumé by sex.		Totals.
		Below 5 years.		5 to 10 years.		10 to 15 years.		15 to 20 years.		20 to 60 years.		Over 60 years.				
	No.	M.	F.	M.	F.	M.	F.	M.	F.	M.	F.	M.	F.	M.	F.	
1. Big Cypress....	10	4	5	a2	2	10	4	9	2	15	b15	2	3	42	31	73
2. Miami River ..	5	5	4	4	4	5	3	7	5	10	13	1	2	32	31	63
3. Fish Eating Creek.	4	a1	1	.....	2	a2	....	3	1	a5	ab10	4	3	15	17	32
4. Cow Creek	1	2	1	.....	....	1	....	....	1	4	3	....	....	7	5	12
5. Cat Fish Lake ..	2	.....	2	3	2	4	1	4	1	a4	ab5	1	1	16	12	28
Totals ..... {		12	13	9	10	22	8	23	10	38	46	8	9	112	96	208
	22	25		19		30		33		84		17		208		

a One mixed blood.   b One black.

Or, for the whole tribe—

Males under 10 years of age... 21
Males between 10 and 20 years of age................................. 45
Males between 20 and 60 years of age................................. 38
Males over 60 years of age... 8
                                                            —— 112
Females under 10 years of age.. 23
Females between 10 and 20 years of age............................... 18
Females between 20 and 60 years of age............................... 46
Females over 60 years of age... 9
                                                             —— 96

In this table it will be noticed that the total population consists of 112 males and 96 females, an excess of males over females of 16. This excess appears in each of the settlements, excepting that of Fish Eating Creek, a fact the more noteworthy, from its relation to the future of the tribe, since polygamous, or certainly duogamous, marriage generally prevails as a tribal custom, at least at the Miami River and the Cat Fish Lake settlements. It will also be observed that between twenty and sixty years of age, or the ordinary range of married life, there are 38 men and 46 women; or, if the women above fifteen years of age are included as wives for the men over twenty years of age, there are 38 men and 56 women. Now, almost all these 56 women are the wives of the 38 men. Notice, however, the manner in which the children of these people are separated in sex. At present there are, under twenty years of age, 66 boys, and, under fifteen years of age, but 31 girls; or, setting aside the 12 boys who are under five years of age, there are, as future possible husbands and wives, 54 boys between five and twenty years of age and 31 girls under fifteen years of age—an excess of 23 boys. For a polygamous society, this excess in the number of the male sex certainly presents a puzzling problem. The statement I had from some cattlemen in mid-Florida I have thus found true, namely, that the Seminole are producing more men than women. What bearing this peculiarity will have upon the future of these Indians can only be guessed at. It is beyond question, however, that the tribe is increasing in numbers, and increasing in the manner above described.

There is no reason why the tribe should not increase, and increase rapidly, if the growth in numbers be not checked by the non-birth of females. The Seminole have not been at war for more than twenty years. Their numbers are not affected by the attacks of wild animals or noxious reptiles. They are not subject to devastating diseases. But once during the last twenty years, as far as I could learn, has anything like an epidemic afflicted them. Besides, at all the settlements except the northernmost, the one at Cat Fish Lake, there is an abundance of food, both animal and vegetable, easily obtained and easily prepared for eating. The climate in which these Indians live is warm and equable throughout the year. They consequently do not need much clothing or shelter. They are not what would be called intemperate, nor are they licentious. The "sprees" in which they indulge when they make their visits to the white man's settlements are too infrequent to warrant us in classing them as intemperate. Their sexual morality is a matter of common notoriety. The white half-breed does not exist among the Florida Seminole, and nowhere could I learn that the Seminole woman is other than virtuous and modest. The birth of a white half-breed would be followed by the death of the Indian mother at the hands of her own people. The only persons of mixed breed among them are children of Indian fathers by negresses who have been adopted into the tribe. Thus health, climate, food, and personal habits apparently conduce to an increase in numbers. The only explanation I can suggest of the fact that there are at present but 208 Seminole in Florida is that at the close of the last war which the United States Government waged on these Indians there were by no means so many of them left in the State as is popularly supposed. As it is, there are now but 17 persons of the tribe over sixty years of age, and no unusual mortality has occurred, certainly among the adults, during the last twenty years. Of the 84 persons between twenty and sixty years of age, the larger number are less than forty years old; and under twenty years of age there are 107 persons, or more than half the whole population. The population tables of the Florida Indians present, therefore, some facts upon which it may be interesting to speculate.

CHAPTER I.

PERSONAL CHARACTERISTICS.

It will be convenient for me to describe the Florida Seminole as they present themselves, first as individuals, and next as members of a society. I know it is impossible to separate, really, the individual as such from the individual as a member of society; nevertheless, there is the man as we see him, having certain characteristics which we call personal, or his own, whencesoever derived, having a certain physique and certain distinguishing psychical qualities. As such I will first attempt to describe the Seminole. Then we shall be able the better to look at him as he is in his relations with his fellows: in the family, in the community, or in any of the forms of the social life of his tribe.

PHYSICAL CHARACTERISTICS.

PHYSIQUE OF THE MEN.

Physically both men and women are remarkable. The men, as a rule, attract attention by their height, fullness and symmetry of development, and the regularity and agreeableness of their features. In muscular power and constitutional ability to endure they excel. While these qualities distinguish, with a few exceptions, the men of the whole tribe, they are particularly characteristic of the two most widely spread of the families of which the tribe is composed. These are the Tiger and Otter clans, which, proud of their lines of descent, have been preserved through a long and tragic past with exceptional freedom from admixture with degrading blood. To-day their men might be taken as types of physical excellence. The physique of every Tiger warrior especially I met would furnish proof of this statement. The Tigers are dark, copper-colored fellows, over six feet in height, with limbs in good proportion; their hands and feet well shaped and not very large; their stature erect; their bearing a sign of self-confident power; their movements deliberate, persistent, strong. Their heads are large, and their foreheads full and marked. An almost universal characteristic of the Tiger's face is its squareness, a widened and protruding under-jawbone giving this effect to it. Of other features, I noticed that under a large forehead are deep set, bright, black eyes, small, but expressive of inquiry and vigilance; the nose is slightly aquiline and sensitively formed about the nostrils; the lips are mobile, sensuous, and not very full, disclosing, when they smile, beautiful regular teeth; and the whole face is expressive of the man's sense of having extraordinary ability to endure and to achieve. Two of the warriors permitted me to manipulate the muscles of their bodies. Under my touch these were more like rubber than flesh. Notice- able among all are the large calves of their legs, the size of the tendons of their lower limbs, and the strength of their toes. I attribute this ex- ceptional development to the fact that they are not what we would call "horse Indians" and that they hunt barefoot over their wide domain. The same causes, perhaps, account for the only real deformity I noticed in the Seminole physique, namely, the diminutive toe-nails, and for the heavy, cracked, and seamed skin which covers the soles of their feet. The feet being otherwise well formed, the toes have only narrow shells for nails, these lying sunken across the middles of the tough cushions of flesh, which, protuberant about them, form the toe-tips. But, regarded as a whole, in their physique the Seminole warriors, especially the men of the Tiger and Otter gentes, are admirable. Even among the children this physical superiority is seen. To illustrate, one morning Ko-i-ha-tco's son, Tin-fai-yai-ki, a tall, slender boy, not quite twelve years old, shouldered a heavy "Kentucky" rifle, left our camp, and followed in his father's long footsteps for a day's hunt. After tramping all day, at sunset he reap- peared in the camp, carrying slung across his shoulders, in addition to rifle and accouterments, a deer weighing perhaps fifty pounds, a weight he had borne for miles. The same boy, in one day, went with some older friends to his permanent home, 20 miles away, and returned. There are, as I have said, exceptions to this rule of unusual physical size and strength, but these are few; so few that, disregarding them, we may pronounce the Seminole men handsome and exceptionally powerful.

PHYSIQUE OF THE WOMEN.

The women to a large extent share the qualities of the men. Some are proportionally tall and handsome, though, curiously enough, many, perhaps a majority, are rather under than over the average height of women. As a rule, they exhibit great bodily vigor. Large or small, they possess regular and agreeable features, shapely and well developed bodies, and they show themselves capable of long continued and severe physical exertion. Indeed, the only Indian women I have seen with at- tractive features and forms are among the Seminole. I would even venture to select from among these Indians three persons whom I could, without much fear of contradiction, present as types respectively of a handsome, a pretty, and a comely woman. Among American Indians, I am confident that the Seminole women are of the first rank.

CLOTHING.

But how is this people clothed? While the clothing of the Seminole is simple and scanty, it is ample for his needs and suitable to the life he leads. The materials of which the clothing is made are now chiefly fabrics manufactured by the white man : calico, cotton cloth, ginghams, and sometimes flannels. They also use some materials prepared by themselves, as deer and other skins. Of ready made articles for wear found in the white trader's store, they buy small woolen shawls, brilliantly colored cotton handkerchiefs, now and then light woolen blankets, and sometimes, lately, though very seldom, shoes.

COSTUME OF THE MEN.

The costume of the Seminole warrior at home consists of a shirt, a neckerchief, a turban, a breech cloth, and, very rarely, moccasins. On but one Indian in camp did I see more than this; on many, less. The shirt is made of some figured or striped cotton cloth, generally of quiet colors. It hangs from the neck to the knees, the narrow, rolling collar being closely buttoned about the neck, the narrow wristbands of the roomy sleeves buttoned about the wrists. The garment opens in front for a few inches, downward from the collar, and is pocketless. A belt of leather or buckskin usually engirdles the man's waist, and from it are suspended one or more pouches, in which powder, bullets, pocket knife, a piece of flint, a small quantity of paper, and like things for use in hunting are carried. From the belt hang also one or more hunting knives, each

FIG. 61. Seminole costume.

nearly 10 inches in length. I questioned one of the Indians about having no pockets in his shirt, pointing out to him the wealth in this respect of the white man's garments, and tried to show him how, on his shirt, as on mine, these convenient receptacles could be placed, and to what straits he was put to carry his pipe, money, and trinkets. He showed little interest in my proposed improvement on his dress.

Having no pockets, the Seminole is obliged to submit to several inconveniences; for instance, he wears his handkerchief about his neck. I have seen as many as six, even eight, handkerchiefs tied around his throat, their knotted ends pendant over his breast; as a rule, they are bright red and yellow things, of whose possession and number he is quite proud. Having no pockets, the Seminole, only here and there one excepted, carries whatever money he obtains from time to time in a knotted corner of one or more of his handkerchiefs.

The next article of the man's ordinary costume is the turban. This is a remarkable structure and gives to its wearer much of his unique appearance. At present it is made of one or more small shawls. These shawls are generally woolen and copied in figure and color from the plaid of some Scotch clan. They are so folded that they are about 3 inches wide and as long as the diagonal of the fabric. They are then, one or more of them successively, wrapped tightly around the head, the top of the head remaining bare ; the last end of the last shawl is tucked skillfully and firmly away, without the use of pins, somewhere in the many folds of the turban. The structure when finished looks like a section of a decorated cylinder crowded down upon the man's head. I

FIG. 62. Key West Billy.

examined one of these turbans and found it a rather firm piece of work, made of several shawls wound into seven concentric rings. It was over 20 inches in diameter, the shell of the cylinder being perhaps 7 inches thick and 3 in width. This head-dress, at the southern settlements, is regularly worn in the camps and sometimes on the hunt. While hunting, however, it seems to be the general custom for the warriors to go bareheaded. At the northern camps, a kerchief bound about the head frequently takes the place of the turban in everyday life, but on dress or festival occasions, at both the northern and the southern settlements, this curious turban is the customary covering for the head of the Seminole brave. Having no pockets in his dress, he has discovered that the folds of his turban may be put to a pocket's uses. Those who use tobacco (I say " those " because the tobacco habit is by no means universal among the red men of Florida) frequently carry their pipes and other articles in their turbans.

When the Seminole warrior makes his rare visits to the white man's settlements, he frequently adds to his scanty camp dress leggins and moccasins.

In the camps I saw but one Indian wearing leggins (Fig. 62); he, however, is in every way a peculiar character among his people, and is objectionably favorable to the white man and the white man's ways.

He is called by the white men " Key West Billy," having received this name because he once made a voyage in a canoe out of the Everglades and along the line of keys south of the Florida mainland to Key West, where he remained for some time. The act itself was so extraordinary, and it was so unusual for a Seminole to enter a white man's town and remain there for any length of time, that a commemorative name was bestowed upon him. The materials of which the leggins of the Seminole are usually made is buckskin. I saw, however, one pair of leggins made of a bright red flannel, and ornamented along the outer seams with a blue and white cross striped braid. The moccasins, also, are made of buckskin, of either a yellow or dark red color. They are made to lace high about the lower part of the leg, the lacing running from below the instep upward. As showing what changes are going on among the Seminole, I may mention that a few of them possess shoes, and one is even the owner of a pair of frontier store boots. The blanket is not often worn by the Florida Indians. Occasionally, in their cool weather, a small shawl, of the kind made to do service in the turban, is thrown about the shoulders. Oftener a piece of calico or white cotton cloth, gathered about the neck, becomes the extra protection against mild coolness in their winters.

FIG. 63. Seminole costume.

COSTUME OF THE WOMEN.

The costume of the women is hardly more complex than that of the men. It consists, apparently, of but two garments, one of which, for lack of a better English word, I name a short shirt, the other a long skirt. The shirt is cut quite low at the neck and is just long enough to cover the breasts. Its sleeves are buttoned close about the wrists. The garment is otherwise buttonless, being wide enough at the neck for it to be easily put on or taken off over the head. The conservatism of the Seminole Indian is shown in nothing more clearly than in the use, by the women, of this much abbreviated covering for the upper part of their bodies. The women are noticeably modest, yet it does not seem to have occurred to them that by making a slight change in their upper garment they might free themselves from frequent embarrassment. In going about their work they were constantly engaged in what our street boys would call " pulling down their vests." This may have been done because a stranger's eyes were upon them ; but I noticed that in rising or in sitting down, or at work, it was a perpetually renewed effort on their part to lengthen by a pull the scanty covering hanging over their breasts. Gathered about the waist is the other garment, the skirt, extending to the feet and often touching the ground. This is usually made of some dark colored calico or gingham. The cord by which the petticoat is fastened is often drawn so tightly about the waist that it gives to that part of the body a rather uncomfortable appearance. This is especially noticeable because the shirt is so short that a space of two or more inches on the body is left uncovered between it and the skirt. I saw no woman wearing moccasins, and I was told that the women never wear them. For headwear the women have nothing, unless the cotton cloth, or small shawl, used about the shoulders in cool weather, and which at times is thrown or drawn over the head, may be called that. (Fig. 63.)

Girls from seven to ten years old are clothed with only a petticoat, and boys about the same age wear only a shirt. Younger children are, as a rule, entirely naked. If clothed at any time, it is only during exceptionally cool weather or when taken by their parents on a journey to the homes of the palefaces.

PERSONAL ADORNMENT.

The love of personal adornment shows itself among the Seminole as among other human beings.

HAIR DRESSING.

The coarse, brilliant, black hair of which they are possessors is taken care of in an odd manner. The men cut all their hair close to the head,

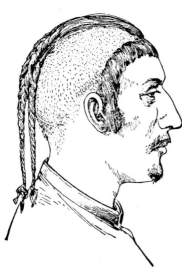

except a strip about an inch wide, running over the front of the scalp from temple to temple, and another strip, of about the same width, perpendicular to the former, crossing the crown of the head to the nape of the neck. At each temple a heavy tuft is allowed to hang to the bottom of the lobe of the ear. The long hair of the strip crossing to the neck is generally gathered and braided into two ornamental queues. I did not learn that these Indians are in the habit of plucking the hair from their faces. I noticed, however, that the moustache is commonly worn among them and that a few of them are endowed with a rather bold looking combination of moustache and imperial. As an exception

FIG. 64. Manner of wearing the hair.

to the uniform style of cutting the hair of the men, I recall the comical appearance of a small negro half breed at the Big Cypress Swamp.

His brilliant wool was twisted into many little sharp cones, which stuck out over his head like so many spikes on an ancient battle club. For some reason there seems to be a much greater neglect of the care of the hair, and, indeed, of the whole person, in the northern than in the southern camps.

The women dress their hair more simply than the men. From a line crossing the head from ear to ear, the hair is gathered up and bound, just above the neck, into a knot somewhat like that often made by the civilized woman, the Indian woman's hair being wrought more into the shape of a cone, sometimes quite elongated and sharp at the apex. A piece of bright ribbon is commonly used at the end as a finish to the structure. The front hair hangs down over the forehead and along the cheeks in front of the ears, being what we call "banged." The only exception to this style of hair dressing I saw was the manner in which Ci-ha-ne, a negress, had disposed of her long crisp tresses. Hers was a veritable Medusa head. A score or more of dangling, snaky plaits, hanging down over her black face and shoulders gave her a most repulsive appearance. Among the little Indian girls the hair is simply braided into a queue and tied with a ribbon, as we often see the hair upon the heads of our school children.

ORNAMENTATION OF CLOTHING.

The clothing of both men and women is ordinarily more or less ornamented. Braids and strips of cloth of various colors are used and wrought upon the garments into odd and sometimes quite tasteful shapes. The upper parts of the shirts of the women are usually embroidered with yellow, red, and brown braids. Sometimes as many as five of these braids lie side by side, parallel with the upper edge of the garment or dropping into a sharp angle between the shoulders. Occasionally a very narrow cape, attached, I think, to the shirt, and much ornamented with braids or stripes, hangs just over the shoulders and back. The same kinds of material used for ornamenting the shirt are also used in decorating the skirt above the lower edge of the petticoat. The women embroider along this edge, with their braids and the narrow colored stripes, a border of diamond and square shaped figures, which is often an elaborate decoration to the dress. In like manner many of the shirts of the men are made pleasing to the eye. I saw no ornamentation in curves: it was always in straight lines and angles.

USE OF BEADS.

My attention was called to the remarkable use of beads among these Indian women, young and old. It seems to be the ambition of the Seminole squaws to gather about their necks as many strings of beads as can be hung there and as they can carry. They are particular as to the quality of the beads they wear. They are satisfied with nothing meaner than a cut glass bead, about a quarter of an inch or more in length, generally of some shade of blue, and costing (so I was told by a trader at Miami) $1.75 a pound. Sometimes, but not often, one sees beads of an inferior quality worn.

These beads must be burdensome to their wearers. In the Big Cypress Swamp settlement one day, to gratify my curiosity as to how many strings of beads these women can wear, I tried to count those worn by " Young Tiger Tail's " wife, number one, Mo-ki, who had come through the Everglades to visit her relatives. She was the proud wearer of certainly not fewer than two hundred strings of good sized beads. She had six quarts (probably a peck of the beads) gathered about her neck, hanging down her back, down upon her breasts, filling the space under her chin, and covering her neck up to her ears. It was an effort for her to move her head. She, however, was only a little, if any, better off in her possessions than most of the others. Others were about equally burdened. Even girl babies are favored by their proud mammas with a varying quantity of the coveted neck wear. The cumbersome beads are said to be worn by night as well as by day.

SILVER DISKS.

Conspicuous among the other ornaments worn by women are silver disks, suspended in a curve across the shirt fronts, under and below the

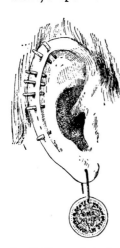

beads. As many as ten or more are worn by one woman. These disks are made by men, who may be called "jewelers to the tribe," from silver quarters and half dollars. The pieces of money are pounded quite thin, made concave, pierced with holes, and ornamented by a groove lying just inside the circumference. Large disks made from half dollars may be called " breast shields." They are suspended, one over each breast. Among the disks other ornaments are often suspended. One young woman I noticed gratifying her vanity with not only eight disks made of silver quarters, but also with three polished copper rifle shells, one bright brass thimble, and a buckle hanging among them. Of course the possession of these and like treasures depends upon the ability and desire of one and another to secure them.

FIG. 65. Manner of piercing the ear.

EAR RINGS.

Ear rings are not generally worn by the Seminole. Those worn are usually made of silver and are of home manufacture. The ears of most of the Indians, however, appear to be pierced, and, as a rule, the ears of the women are pierced many times; for what purpose I did not discover. Along and in the upper edges of the ears of the women from one to ten or more small holes have been made. In most of these holes

I noticed bits of palmetto wood, about a fifth of an inch in length and in diameter the size of a large pin. Seemingly they were not placed there to remain only while the puncture was healing. (Fig. 65.)

Piercing the ears excepted, the Florida Indians do not now mutilate their bodies for beauty's sake. They no longer pierce the lips or the nose; nor do they use paint upon their persons, I am told, except at their great annual festival, the Green Corn Dance, and upon the faces of their dead.

FINGER RINGS.

Nor is the wearing of finger rings more common than that of rings for the ears. The finger rings I saw were all made of silver and showed good workmanship. Most of them were made with large elliptical tablets on them, extending from knuckle to knuckle. These also were home-made.

SILVER VS. GOLD.

I saw no gold ornaments. Gold, even gold money, does not seem to be considered of much value by the Seminole. He is a monometalist, and his precious metal is silver. I was told by a cattle dealer of an Indian who once gave him a twenty dollar gold piece for $17 in silver, although assured that the gold piece was worth more than the silver, and in my own intercourse with the Seminole I found them to manifest, with few exceptions, a decided preference for silver. I was told that the Seminole are peculiar in wishing to possess nothing that is not genuine of its apparent kind. Traders told me that, so far as the Indians know, they will buy of them only what is the best either of food or of material for wear or ornament.

CRESCENTS, WRISTLETS, AND BELTS.

The ornaments worn by the men which are most worthy of attention are crescents, varying in size and value. These are generally about five inches long, an inch in width at the widest part, and of the thickness of ordinary tin. These articles are also made from silver coins and are of home manufacture. They are worn suspended from the neck by cords, in the cusps of the crescents, one below another, at distances apart of perhaps two and a half inches. Silver wristlets are used by the men for their adornment. They are fastened about the wrists by cords or thongs passing through holes in the ends of the metal. Belts, and turbans too, are often ornamented with fanciful devices wrought out of silver. It is not customary for the Indian men to wear these ornaments in everyday camp life. They appear with them on a festival occasion or when they visit some trading post.

ME-LE.

A sketch made by Lieutenant Brown, of Saint Francis Barracks, Saint Augustine, Florida, who accompanied me on my trip to the Cat

Fish Lake settlement, enables me to show, in gala dress, Me-le, a half breed Seminole, the son of an Indian, Ho-laq-to-mik-ko, by a negress adopted into the tribe when a child.

Me-le sat for his picture in my room at a hotel in Orlando. He had just come seventy miles from his home, at Cat Fish Lake, to see the white man and a white man's town. He was clothed "in his best," and, moreover, had just purchased and was wearing a pair of store boots in addition to his home-made finery. He was the owner of the one pair of red flannel leggins of which I have spoken. These were not long enough to cover the brown skin of his sturdy thighs. His ornaments were silver crescents, wristlets, a silver studded belt, and a peculiar battlement-like band of silver on the edge of his turban. Notice his uncropped head of luxuriant, curly hair, the only exception I observed to the singular cut of hair peculiar to the Seminole men. Me-le, however, is in many other more important respects an exceptional character. He is not at all in favor with the Seminole of pure blood. "Me-le ho-lo-wa kis" (Me-le is of no account) was the judgment passed upon him to me by some of the Indians. Why? Because he likes the white man and would live the white man's life if he knew how to break away safely from his tribe. He has been progressive enough to build for himself a frame house, inclosed on all sides and entered by a door. More than that, he is not satisfied with the hunting habits and the simple agriculture of his people, nor with their ways of doing other things. He has started an orange grove, and in a short time will have a hundred trees, so he says, bearing fruit. He has bought and uses a sewing machine, and he was intelligent enough, so the report goes, when the machine had been taken to pieces in his presence, to put it together again without mistake. He once called off for me from a newspaper the names of the letters of our alphabet, and legibly wrote his English name, "John Willis Mik-ko." Mik-ko has a restless, inquisitive mind, and deserves the notice and care of those who are interested in the progress of this people. Seeking him one day at Orlando, I found him busily studying the locomotive engine of the little road which had been pushed out into that part of the frontier of Florida's civilized population. Next morning he was at the station to see the train depart, and told me he would like to go with me to Jacksonville. He is the only Florida Seminole, I believe, who had at that time seen a railway.

PSYCHICAL CHARACTERISTICS.

I shall now glance at what may more properly be called the psychical characteristics of the Florida Indians. I have been led to the conclusion that for Indians they have attained a relatively high degree of psychical development. They are an uncivilized, I hardly like to call them a savage, people. They are antagonistic to white men, as a race, and to the white man's culture, but they have characteristics of their own, many of which are commendable. They are decided in their enmity to any representative of the white man's government and to every thing which bears upon it the government's mark. To one, however, who is acquainted with recent history this enmity is but natural, and a confessed representative of the government need not be surprised at finding in the Seminole only forbidding and unlovely qualities. But when suspicion is disarmed, one whom they have welcomed to their confidence will find them evincing characteristics which will excite his admiration and esteem. I was fortunate enough to be introduced to the Seminole, not as a representative of our National Government, but under conditions which induced them to welcome me as a friend. In my intercourse with them, I found them to be not only the brave, self reliant, proud people who have from time to time withstood our nation's armies in defense of their rights, but also a people amiable, affectionate, truthful, and communicative. Nor are they devoid of a sense of humor. With only few exceptions, I found them genial. Indeed, the old chief, Tûs-te-nûg-ge, a man whose warwhoop and deadly hand, during the last half century, have often been heard and felt among the Florida swamps and prairies, was the only one disposed to sulk in my presence and to repel friendly advances. He called me to him when I entered the camp where he was, and, with great dignity of manner, asked after my business among his people. After listening, through my interpreter, to my answers to his questions, he turned from me and honored me no further. I call the Seminole communicative, because most with whom I spoke were eager to talk, and, as far as they could with the imperfect means at their disposal, to give me the information I sought. " Doctor Na-ki-ta " (Doctor What-is-it) I was playfully named at the Cat Fish Lake settlement; yet the people there were seemingly as ready to try to answer as I was to ask, " What is it ? " I said they are truthful. That is their reputation with many of the white men I met, and I have reason to believe that the reputation is under ordinary circumstances well founded. They answered promptly and without equivocation " No" or " Yes " or " I don't know." And they are affectionate to one another, and, so far as I saw, amiable in their domestic and social intercourse. Parental affection is characteristic of their home life, as several illustrative instances I might mention would show. I will mention one. Täl-la-häs-ke is the father of six fine looking boys, ranging in age from four to eighteen years. Seven months before I met him his wife died, and when I was at his camp this strong Indian appeared to have become both mother and father to his children. His solicitous affection seemed continually to follow these boys, watching their movements and caring for their comfort. Especially did he throw a tender care about the little one of his household. I have seen this little fellow clambering, just like many a little paleface, over his father's knees and back, persistently demanding attention but in no way disturbing the father's amiability or serenity, even while the latter was trying to oblige me by answering puzzling questions upon matters connected with his tribe. One night, as Lieutenant Brown and I sat by the campfire at Täl-la-häs-ke's lodge — the larger boys, two Seminole negresses, three pigs, and several dogs, together with Täl-la-häs-ke, forming a picturesque circle in the ashes around the bright light — I heard muffled moans from the little palmetto shelter on my right, under which the three smaller boys were bundled up in cotton cloth on deer skins for the night's sleep. Upon the moans followed immediately the frightened cry of the baby boy, waking out of bad dreams and crying for the mother who could not answer; "Its-ki, Its-ki" (mother, mother) begged the little fellow, struggling from under his covering. At once the big Indian grasped his child, hugged him to his breast, pressed the little head to his cheek, consoling him all the while with caressing words, whose meaning I felt, though I could not have translated them into English, until the boy, wide awake, laughed with his father and us all and was ready to be again rolled up beside his sleeping brothers. I have said also that the Seminole are frank. Formal or hypocritical courtesy does not characterize them. One of my party wished to accompany Ka-tca-la-ni ("Yellow Tiger") on a hunt. He wished to see how the Indian would find, approach, and capture his game. "Me go hunt with you, Tom, to-day?" asked our man. "No," answered Tom, and in his own language continued, "not to-day; to-morrow." To-morrow came, and, with it, Tom to our camp. "You can go to Horse Creek with me; then I hunt alone and you come back," was the Indian's remark as both set out. I afterwards learned that Ka-tca-la-ni was all kindness on the trail to Horse Creek, three miles away, aiding the amateur hunter in his search for game and giving him the first shot at what was started. At Horse Creek, however, Tom stopped, and, turning to his companion, said, "Now you hi-e-pus (go)!" That was frankness indeed, and quite refreshing to us who had not been honored by it. But equally outspoken, without intending offense, I found them always. You could not mistake their meaning, did you understand their words. Diplomacy seems, as yet, to be an unlearned art among them.

KO-NIP-HA-TCO.

Here is another illustration of their frankness. One Indian, Ko-nip-ha-tco ("Billy"), a brother of "Key West Billy," has become so desirous of identifying himself with the white people that in 1879 he came to Capt. F. A. Hendry, at Myers, and asked permission to live with him. Permission was willingly given, and when I went to Florida this "Billy" had been studying our language and ways for more than a year. At that time he was the only Seminole who had separated himself from his people and had cast in his lot with the whites. He had clothed himself in our dress and taken to the bed and table, instead of the ground and kettle, for sleep and food. "Me all same white man," he boastfully told me one day. But

I will not here relate the interesting story of "Billy's" previous life or of his adventures in reaching his present proud position. It is sufficient to say that, for the time at least, he had become in the eyes of his people a member of a foreign community. As may be easily guessed, Ko-nip-ha-tco's act was not at all looked upon with favor by the Indians; it was, on the contrary, seriously opposed. Several tribal councils made him the subject of discussion, and once, during the year before I met him, five of his relatives came to Myers and compelled him to return with them for a time to his home at the Big Cypress Swamp. But to my illustration of Seminole frankness: In the autumn of 1880, Mat-te-lo, a prominent Seminole, was at Myers and happened to meet Captain Hendry. While they stood together "Billy" passed. Hardly had the young fellow disappeared when Mat-te-lo said to Captain Hendry, "Bum-by, Indian kill Billy." But an answer came. In this case the answer of the white man was equally frank: "Mat-te-lo, when Indian kill Billy, white man kill Indian, remember." And so the talk ended, the Seminole looking hard at the captain to try to discover whether he had meant what he said.

INTELLECTUAL ABILITY.

In range of intellectual power and mental processes the Florida Indians, when compared with the intellectual abilities and operations of the cultivated American, are quite limited. But if the Seminole are to be judged by comparison with other American aborigines, I believe they easily enter the first class. They seem to be mentally active. When the full expression of any of my questions failed, a substantive or two, an adverb, and a little pantomime generally sufficed to convey the meaning to my hearers. In their intercourse with one another, they are, as a rule, voluble, vivacious, showing the possession of relatively active brains and mental fertility. Certainly, most of the Seminole I met cannot justly be called either stupid or intellectually sluggish, and I observed that, when invited to think of matters with which they are not familiar or which are beyond the verge of the domain which their intellectual faculties have mastered, they nevertheless bravely endeavored to satisfy me before they were willing to acknowledge themselves powerless. They would not at once answer a misunderstood or unintelligible question, but would return inquiry upon inquiry, before the decided " I don't know" was uttered. Those with whom I particularly dealt were exceptionally patient under the strains to which I put their minds. Ko-nip-ha-tco, by no means a brilliant member of his tribe, is much to be commended for his patient, persistent, intellectual industry. I kept the young fellow busy for about a fortnight, from half-past eight in the morning until five in the afternoon, with but an hour and a half's intermission at noon. Occupying our time with inquiries not very interesting to him, about the language and life of his people, I could see how much I wearied him. Often I found by his answers that his brain was, to a degree, paralyzed by the long continued tension to which it was subjected. But he held on bravely through the severe heat of an attic room at Myers. Despite the insects, myriads of which took a great interest in us and our surroundings, despite the persistent invitation of the near woods to him to leave " Doctor Na-ki-ta" and to tramp off in them on a deer hunt (for "Billy" is a lover of the woods and a bold and successful hunter), he held on courageously. The only sign of weakening he made was on one day, about noon, when, after many, to me, vexatious failures to draw from him certain translations into his own language of phrases containing verbs illustrating variations of mood, time, number, &c., he said to me: " Doctor, how long you want me to tell you Indian language?" " Why?" I replied, " are you tired, Billy?" "No," he answered, "a littly. Me think me tell you all. Me don't know English language. Bum-by you come, next winter, me tell you all. Me go school. Me learn. Me go hunt deer to-mollow." I was afraid of losing my hold upon him, for time was precious. " Billy," I said, "you go now. You hunt to-day. I need you just three days more and then you can hunt all the time. To-morrow come, and I will ask you easier questions." After only a moment's hesitation, "Me no go, Doctor; me stay," was his courageous decision.

CHAPTER II.

SEMINOLE SOCIETY.

As I now direct attention to the Florida Seminole in their relations with one another, I shall first treat of that relationship which lies at the foundation of society, marriage or its equivalent, the result of which is a body of people more or less remotely connected with one another and designated by the term "kindred." This is shown either in the narrow limits of what may be named the family or in the larger bounds of what is called the clan or gens. I attempted to get full insight into the system of relationships in which Seminole kinship is embodied, and, while my efforts were not followed by an altogether satisfactory result, I saw enough to enable me to say that the Seminole relationships are essentially those of what we may call their "mother tribe," the Creek. The Florida Seminole are a people containing, to some extent, the posterity of tribes diverse from the Creek in language and in social and political organization; but so strong has the Creek influence been in their development that the Creek language, Creek customs, and Creek regulations have been the guiding forces in their history, forces by which, in fact, the characteristics of the other peoples have yielded, have been practically obliterated.

I have made a careful comparison of the terms of Seminole relationship I obtained with those of the Creek Indians, embodied in Dr. L. H. Morgan's Consanguinity and Affinity of the American Indians, and I find that, as far as I was able to go, they are the same, allowing for the natural differences of pronunciation of the two peoples. The only seeming difference of relationships lies in the names applied to some of the lineal descendants, descriptive instead of classificatory names being used.

I have said, "as far as I was able to go." I found, for example, that beyond the second collateral line among consanguineous kindred my interpreter would answer my question only by some such answer as "I don't know" or "No kin," and that, beyond the first collateral line of kindred by marriage, except for a very few relationships, I could obtain no answer.

THE SEMINOLE FAMILY.

The family consists of the husband, one or more wives, and their children. I do not know what limit tribal law places to the number of wives the Florida Indian may have, but certainly he may possess two. There are several Seminole families in which duogamy exists.

COURTSHIP.

I learned the following facts concerning the formation of a family: A young warrior, at the age of twenty or less, sees an Indian maiden of about sixteen years, and by a natural impulse desires to make her his wife. What follows? He calls his immediate relatives to a council and tells them of his wish. If the damsel is not a member of the lover's own gens and if no other impediment stands in the way of the proposed alliance, they select, from their own number, some who, at an appropriate time, go to the maiden's kindred and tell them that they desire the maid to receive their kinsman as her husband. The girl's relatives then consider the question. If they decide in favor of the union, they interrogate the prospective bride as to her disposition towards the young man. If she also is willing, news of the double consent is conveyed through the relatives, on both sides, to the prospective husband. From that moment there is a gentle excitement in both households. The female relatives of the young man take to the house of the betrothed's mother a blanket or a large piece of cotton cloth and a bed canopy—in other words, the furnishing of a new bed. Thereupon there is returned thence to the young man a wedding costume, consisting of a newly made shirt.

MARRIAGE.

Arrangements for the marriage being thus completed, the marriage takes place by the very informal ceremony of the going of the bridegroom, at sunset of an appointed day, to the home of his mother-in-law, where he is received by his bride. From that time he is her husband. The next day, husband and wife appear together in the camp, and are thenceforth recognized as a wedded pair. After the marriage, through what is the equivalent of the white man's honeymoon, and often for a much longer period, the new couple remain at the home of the mother-in-law. It is the man and not the woman among these Indians who leaves father and mother and cleaves unto the mate. After a time, especially as the family increases, the wedded pair build one or more houses for independent housekeeping, either at the camp of the wife's mother or elsewhere, excepting among the husband's relatives.

DIVORCE.

The home may continue until death breaks it up. Sometimes, however, it occurs that most hopeful matrimonial beginnings, among the Florida Seminole, as elsewhere, end in disappointment and ruin. How divorce is accomplished I could not learn. I pressed the question upon Ko-nip-ha-tco, but his answer was, "Me don't know; Indian no tell me much." All the light I obtained upon the subject comes from Billy's first reply, "He left her." In fact, desertion seems to be the only ceremony accompanying a divorce. The husband, no longer satisfied with his wife, leaves her; she returns to her family, and the matter is ended.

There is no embarrassment growing out of problems respecting the woman's future support, the division of property, or the adjustment of claims for the possession of the children. The independent self-support of every adult, healthy Indian, female as well as male, and the gentile relationship, which is more wide reaching and authoritative than that of marriage, have already disposed of these questions, which are usually so perplexing for the white man. So far as personal maintenance is concerned, a woman is, as a rule, just as well off without a husband as with one. What is hers, in the shape of property, remains her own whether she is married or not. In fact, marriage among these Indians seems to be but the natural mating of the sexes, to cease at the option of either of the interested parties. Although I do not know that the wife may lawfully desert her husband, as well as the husband his wife, from some facts learned I think it probable that she may.

CHILDBIRTH.

According to information received a prospective mother, as the hour of her confinement approaches, selects a place for the birth of her child not far from the main house of the family, and there, with some friends, builds a small lodge, covering the top and sides of the structure generally with the large leaves of the cabbage palmetto. To this secluded place the woman, with some elderly female relatives, goes at the time the child is to be born, and there, in a sitting posture, her hands grasping a strong stick driven into the ground before her, she is delivered of her babe, which is received and cared for by her companions. Rarely is the Indian mother's labor difficult or followed by a prolonged sickness. Usually she returns to her home with her little one within four days after its birth.

INFANCY.

The baby, well into the world, learns very quickly that he is to make his own way through it as best he may. His mother is prompt to nourish him and solicitous in her care for him if he falls ill, but, as far as possible, she goes her own way and leaves the little fellow to go his.

Fig. 66. Baby cradle or hammock.

From the first she gives her child the perfectly free use of his body and, within a limited area, of the camp ground. She does not bundle him into a motionless thing or bind him helplessly on a board; on the contrary, she does not trouble her child even with clothing. The Florida Indian baby, when very young, spends his time, naked, in a hammock, or on a deer skin, or on the warm earth. (Fig. 66.)

The Seminole mother, I was informed, is not in the habit of soothing her baby with song. Nevertheless, sometimes one may hear her or an old grandam crooning a monotonous refrain as she crouches on the ground beside the swinging hammock of a baby. I heard one of these refrains, and, as nearly as I could catch it, it ran thus:

No-wut-tca, No-wut-tca.

The hammock was swung in time with the song. The singing was slow in movement and nasal in quality. The last note was unmusical and uttered quite staccato.

There are times, to be sure, when the Seminole mother carries her baby. He is not always left to his pleasure on the ground or in a hammock. When there is no little sister or old grandmother to look after the helpless creature and the mother is forced to go to any distance from her house or lodge, she takes him with her. This she does, usually, by setting him astride one of her hips and holding him there. If she wishes to have both her arms free, however, she puts the baby into the center of a piece of cotton cloth, ties opposite corners of the cloth together, and slings her burden over her shoulders and upon her back, where, with his brown legs astride his mother's hips, the infant rides, generally with much satisfaction. I remember seeing, one day, one jolly little fellow, lolling and rollicking on his mother's back, kicking her and tugging away at the strings of beads which hung temptingly between her shoulders, while the mother, hand-free, bore on one shoulder a log, which, a moment afterwards, still keeping her baby on her back as she did so, she chopped into small wood for the camp fire.

CHILDHOOD.

But just as soon as the Seminole baby has gained sufficient strength to toddle he learns that the more he can do for himself and the more he can contribute to the general domestic welfare the better he will get along in life. No small amount of the labor in a Seminole household is done by children, even as young as four years of age. They can stir the soup while it is boiling; they can aid in kneading the dough for bread; they can wash the "Koonti" root, and even pound it; they can watch and replenish the fire; they contribute in this and many other small ways to the necessary work of the home. I am not to be understood, of course, as saying that the little Seminole's life is one of severe labor. He has plenty of time for games and play of all kinds, and of these I shall hereafter speak. Yet, as soon as he is able to play, he finds that with his play he must mix work in considerable measure.

SEMINOLE DWELLINGS—I-FUL-LO-HA-TCO'S HOUSE.

Now that we have seen the Seminole family formed, let us look at its home. The Florida Indians are not nomads. They have fixed habitations: settlements in well defined districts, permanent camps, houses or wigwams which remain from year to year the abiding places of their families, and gardens and fields which for indefinite periods are used by the same owners. There are times during the year when parties gather into temporary camps for a few weeks. Now perhaps they gather upon some rich Koonti ground, that they may dig an extra quantity of this root and make flour from it; now, that they may have a sirup making festival, they go to some fertile sugar cane hammock; or again, that they may have a hunt, they camp where a certain kind of game has been discovered in abundance. And they all, as a rule, go to a central point once a year and share there their great feast, the Green Corn Dance. Besides, as I was told, these Indians are frequent visitors to one another, acting in turn as guests and hosts for a few days at a time. But it is the fact, nevertheless, that for much the greater part of the year the Seminole families are at their homes, occupying houses, surrounded by many comforts and living a life of routine industry.

As one Seminole home is, with but few unimportant differences, like nearly all the others, we can get a good idea of what it is by describing here the first one I visited, that of I-ful-lo-ha-tco, or "Charlie Osceola," in the "Bad Country," on the edge of the Big Cypress Swamp.

When my guide pointed out to me the locality where "Charlie" lives, I could see nothing but a wide saw-grass marsh surrounding a small island. The island seemed covered with a dense growth of palmetto and other trees and tangled shrubbery, with a few banana plants rising among them. No sign of human habitation was visible. This invisibility of a Seminole's house from the vicinity may be taken as a marked characteristic of his home. If possible, he hides his house, placing it on an island and in a jungle. As we neared the hammock we found that approach to it was difficult. On horseback there was no trouble in getting through the water and the annoying saw-grass, but I found it difficult to reach the island with my vehicle, which was loaded with our provisions and myself. On the shore of "Charlie's" island is a piece of rich land of probably two acres in extent. At length I landed, and soon, to my surprise, entered a small, neat clearing, around which were built three houses, excellent of their kind, and one insignificant structure. Beyond these, well fenced with palmetto logs, lay a small garden. No one of the entire household—father, mother, and child—was at home. Where they had gone we did not learn until later. We found them next day at a sirup making at "Old Tommy's" field, six miles away. Having, in the absence of the owner, a free range of the camp, I busied myself in noting what had been left in it and what were its peculiarities. Among the first things I picked up was a "cow's horn."

This, my guide informed me, was used in calling from camp to camp.

Mountin   a pile of logs, "Billy" tried with it to summon "Charlie," thinking he might be somewhere near.   Meanwhile I continued my search.   I noticed some terrapin shells lying on a platform in one of the houses, the breast shell pierced with two holes.   " Wear them at Green Corn Dance," said " Billy."   I caught sight of some dressed buckskins lying on a rafter of a house, and an old fashioned rifle, with powder horn and shot flask.   I also saw a hoe; a deep iron pot; a mortar, made from a live oak (?) log, probably fifteen inches in diameter and twenty-four in height, and beside it a pestle, made from mastic wood, perhaps four feet and a half in length.

A bag of corn hung from a rafter, and near it a sack of clothing, which I did not examine.   A skirt, gayly ornamented, hung there also. There were several basketware sieves, evidently home made, and various bottles lying around the place.   I did not search among the things laid away on the rafters under the roof.   A sow, with several pigs, lay contentedly under the platform of one of the houses.   And near by, in the saw-grass, was moored a cypress "dug-out," about fifteen feet long, pointed at bow and stern.

Dwellings throughout the Seminole district are practically uniform in construction.   With but slight variations, the accompanying sketch of I-ful-lo-ha-tco's main dwelling shows what style of architecture prevails in the Florida Everglades.   (Pl. XIX.)

This house is approximately 16 by 9 feet in ground measurement, made almost altogether, if not wholly, of materials taken from the palmetto tree.   It is actually but a platform elevated about three feet from the ground and covered with a palmetto thatched roof, the roof being not more than 12 feet above the ground at the ridge pole, or 7 at the eaves.   Eight upright palmetto logs, unsplit and undressed, support the roof.   Many rafters sustain the palmetto thatching.   The platform is composed of split palmetto logs lying transversely, flat sides up, upon beams which extend the length of the building and are lashed to the uprights by palmetto ropes, thongs, or trader's ropes.   This platform is peculiar, in that it fills the interior of the building like a floor and serves to furnish the family with a dry sitting or lying down place when, as often happens, the whole region is under water.   The thatching of the roof is quite a work of art: inside, the regularity and compactness of the laying of the leaves display much skill and taste on the part of the builder; outside—with the outer layers there seems to have been less care taken than with those within —the mass of leaves of which the roof is composed is held in place and made firm by heavy logs, which, bound together in pairs, are laid upon it astride the ridge.   The covering is, I was informed, water tight and durable and will resist even a violent wind.   Only hurricanes can tear it off, and these are so infrequent in Southern Florida that no attempt is made to provide against them.

The Seminole's house is open on all sides and without rooms.   It is, in fact, only a covered platform.   The single equivalent for a room in it

SEA-LION HUNTING

is the space above the joists which are extended across the building at the lower edges of the roof. In this are placed surplus food and general household effects out of use from time to time. Household utensils are usually suspended from the uprights of the building and from pronged sticks driven into the ground near by at convenient places.

From this description the Seminole's house may seem a poor kind of structure to use as a dwelling; yet if we take into account the climate of Southern Florida nothing more would seem to be necessary. A shelter from the hot sun and the frequent rains and a dry floor above the damp or water covered ground are sufficient for the Florida Indian's needs.

I-ful-lo-ha-tco's three houses are placed at three corners of an oblong clearing, which is perhaps 40 by 30 feet. At the fourth corner is the entrance into the garden, which is in shape an ellipse, the longer diameter being about 25 feet. The three houses are alike, with the exception that in one of them the elevated platform is only half the size of those of the others. This difference seems to have been made on account of the camp fire. The fire usually burns in the space around which the buildings stand. During the wet season, however, it is moved into the sheltered floor in the building having the half platform. At Tus-ko-na's camp, where several families are gathered, I noticed one building without the interior platform. This was probably the wet weather kitchen.

To all appearance there is no privacy in these open houses. The only means by which it seems to be secured is by suspending, over where one sleeps, a canopy of thin cotton cloth or calico, made square or oblong in shape, and nearly three feet in height. This serves a double use, as a private room and as a protection against gnats and mosquitoes.

But while I-ful-lo ha-tco's house is a fair example of the kind of dwelling in use throughout the tribe, I may not pass unnoticed some innovations which have lately been made upon the general style. There are, I understand, five inclosed houses, which were built and are owned by Florida Indians. Four of these are covered with split cypress planks or slabs; one is constructed of logs.

Progressive " Key West Billy " has gone further than any other one, excepting perhaps Me-le, in the white man's ways of house building. He has erected for his family, which consists of one wife and three children, a cypress board house, and furnished it with doors and windows, partitions, floors, and ceiling. In the house are one upper and one or two lower rooms. Outside, he has a stairway to the upper floor, and from the upper floor a balcony. He possesses also an elevated bed, a trunk for his clothing, and a straw hat.

Besides the permanent home for the Seminole family, there is also the lodge which it occupies when for any cause it temporarily leaves the house. The lodges, or the temporary structures which the Seminole make when "camping out," are, of course, much simpler and less comfortable than their houses. I had the privilege of visiting two "camping" parties—one of forty-eight Indians, at Tak-o- si-mac la's cane field, on the edge of the Big Cypress Swamp; the other of twenty-two persons, at a Koonti ground, on Horse Creek, not far from the site of what was, long ago, Fort Davenport.

I found great difficulty in reaching the "camp" at the sugar cane field. I was obliged to leave my conveyance some distance from the island on which the cane field was located. When we arrived at the shore of the saw-grass marsh no outward sign indicated the presence of fifty Indians so close at hand; but suddenly three turbaned Seminole emerged from the marsh, as we stood there. Learning from our guide our business, they cordially offered to conduct us through the water and saw-grass to the camp. The wading was annoying and, to me, difficult; but at length we secured dry footing in the jungle on the island, and after a tortuous way through the tangled vegetation, which walled in the camp from the prairie, we entered the large clearing and the collection of lodges where the Indians were. These lodges, placed very close together and seemingly without order, were almost all made of white cotton cloths, which were each stretched over ridge poles and tied to four corner posts. The lodges were in shape like the fly of a wall tent, simply a sheet stretched for a cover.

At a Koonti ground on Horse Creek I met the Cat Fish Lake Indians. They had been forced to leave their homes to secure an extra supply of Koonti flour, because, as I understood the woman who told me, some animals had eaten all their sweet potatoes. The lodges of this party differed from those of the southern Indians in being covered above and around with palmetto leaves and in being shaped some like wall tents and others like single-roofed sheds. The accompanying sketch shows what kind of a shelter Täl-la-häs-ke had made for himself at Horse Creek. (Fig. 67.)

FIG. 67. Temporary dwelling.

Adjoining each of these lodges was a platform, breast high. These were made of small poles or sticks covered with the leaves of the palmetto. Upon and under these, food, clothing, and household utensils, generally, were kept; and between the rafters of the lodges and the roofs, also, many articles, especially those for personal use and adornment, were stored.

HOME LIFE.

Having now seen the formation of the Seminole family and taken a glance at the dwellings, permanent and temporary, which it occupies, we are prepared to look at its household life. I was surprised by the industry and comparative prosperity and, further, by the cheerfulness and mutual confidence, intimacy, and affection of these Indians in their family intercourse.

The Seminole family is industrious. All its members work who are able to do so, men as well as women. The former are not only hunters, fishermen, and herders, but agriculturists also. The women not only care for their children and look after the preparation of food and the general welfare of the home, but are, besides, laborers in the fields. In the Seminole family, both husband and wife are land proprietors and cultivators. Moreover, as we have seen, all children able to labor contribute their little to the household prosperity. From these various domestic characteristics, an industrious family life almost necessarily follows. The disesteem in which Tûs-ko-na, a notorious loafer at the Big Cypress Swamp, is held by the other Indians shows that laziness is not countenanced among the Seminole.

But let me not be misunderstood here. By a Seminole's industry I do not mean the persistent and rapid labor of the white man of a northern community. The Indian is not capable of this, nor is he compelled to imitate it. I mean only that, in describing him, it is but just for me to say that he is a worker and not a loafer.

As a result of the domestic industry it would be expected that we should find comparative prosperity prevailing among all Seminole families ; and this is the fact. Much of the Indian's labor is wasted through his ignorance of the ways by which it might be economized. He has no labor saving or labor multiplying machines. There is but little differentiation of function in either family or tribe. Each worker does all kinds of work. Men give themselves to the hunt, women to the house, and both to the field. But men may be found sometimes at the cooking pot or toasting stick and women may be seen taking care of cattle and horses. Men bring home deer and turkeys, &c. ; women spend days in fishing. Both men and women are tailors, shoemakers, flour makers, cane crushers and sirup boilers, wood hewers and bearers, and water carriers. There are but few domestic functions which may be said to belong exclusively, on the one hand, to men, or, on the other, to women.

Out of the diversified domestic industry, as I have said, comes comparative prosperity. The home is all that the Seminole family needs or desires for its comfort. There is enough clothing, or the means to get it, for every one. Ordinarily more than a sufficient quantity of clothes is possessed by each member of a family. No one lacks money or the material with which to obtain that which money purchases. Nor need any ever hunger, since the fields and nature offer them food in abundance. The families of the northern camps are not as well provided for by bountiful nature as those south of the Caloosahatchie River. Yet, though at my visit to the Cat Fish Lake Indians in midwinter the sweet potatoes were all gone, a good hunting ground and fertile fields of Koonti were near at hand for Tcup-ko's people to visit and use to their profit.

FOOD.

Read the bill of fare from which the Florida Indians may select, and compare with that the scanty supplies within reach of the North Carolina Cherokee or the Lake Superior Chippewa. Here is a list of their meats: Of flesh, at any time venison, often opossum, sometimes rabbit and squirrel, occasionally bear, and a land terrapin, called the "gopher," and pork whenever they wish it. Of wild fowl, duck, quail, and turkey in abundance. Of home reared fowl, chickens, more than they are willing to use. Of fish, they can catch myriads of the many kinds which teem in the inland waters of Florida, especially of the large bass, called "trout" by the whites of the State, while on the seashore they can get many forms of edible marine life, especially turtles and oysters. Equally well off are these Indians in respect to grains, vegetables, roots, and fruits. They grow maize in considerable quantity, and from it make hominy and flour, and all the rice they need they gather from the swamps. Their vegetables are chiefly sweet potatoes, large and much praised melons and pumpkins, and, if I may classify it with vegetables, the tender new growth of the tree called the cabbage palmetto. Among roots, there is the great dependence of these Indians, the abounding Koonti; also the wild potato, a small tuber found in black swamp land, and peanuts in great quantities. Of fruits, the Seminole family may supply itself with bananas, oranges (sour and sweet), limes, lemons, guavas, pineapples, grapes (black and red), cocoa nuts, cocoa plums, sea grapes, and wild plums. And with even this enumeration the bill of fare is not exhausted. The Seminole, living in a perennial summer, is never at a loss when he seeks something, and something good, to eat. I have omitted from the above list honey and the sugar cane juice and sirup, nor have I referred to the purchases the Indians now and then make from the white man, of salt pork, wheat flour, coffee, and salt, and of the various canned delicacies, whose attractive labels catch their eyes.

These Indians are not, of course, particularly provident. I was told, however, that they are beginning to be ambitious to increase their little herds of horses and cattle and their numbers of chickens and swine.

CAMP FIRE.

Entering the more interior, the intimate home life of the Seminole, one observes that the center about which it gathers is the camp fire. This is never large except on a cool night, but it is of unceasing interest to the household. It is the place where the food is prepared, and where, by day, it is always preparing. It is the place where the social intercourse of the family, and of the family with their friends, is enjoyed. There the story is told; by its side toilets are made and household duties are performed, not necessarily on account of the warmth the fire gives, for it is often so small that its heat is almost imperceptible, but because of its central position in the household economy. This fire is somewhat singularly constructed; the logs used for it are of considerable length, and are laid, with some regularity, around a center, like the radii of a circle. These logs are pushed directly inward as the inner ends are consumed. The outer ends of the logs make excellent seats; sometimes they serve as pillows, especially for old men and women wishing to take afternoon naps.

Beds and bedding are of far less account to the Seminole family than the camp fire. The bed is often only the place where one chooses to lie. It is generally, however, chosen under the sheltering roof on the elevated platform, or, when made in the lodge, on palmetto leaves. It is pillowless, and has covering or not, as the sleeper may wish. If a cover is used, it is, as a rule, only a thin blanket or a sheet of cotton cloth, besides, during most of the year, the canopy or mosquito bar.

MANNER OF EATING.

Next in importance to the camp fire in the life of the Seminole household naturally comes the eating of what is prepared there. There is nothing very formal in that. The Indians do not set a table or lay dishes and arrange chairs. A good sized kettle, containing stewed meat and vegetables, is the center around which the family gathers for its meal. This, placed in some convenient spot on the ground near the fire, is surrounded by more or fewer of the members of the household in a sitting posture. If all that they have to eat at that time is contained in the kettle, each extracts, with his fingers or his knife, a piece of meat or a bone with meat on it, and, holding it in one hand, eats, while with the other hand each, in turn, supplies himself, by means of a great wooden spoon, from the porridge in the pot.

The Seminole, however, though observing meal times with some regularity, eats just as his appetite invites. If it happens that he has a side of venison roasting before the fire, he will cut from it at any time during the day and, with the piece of meat in one hand and a bit of Koonti or of different bread in the other, satisfy his appetite. Not seldom, too, he rises during the night and breaks his sleep by eating a piece of the roasting meat. The kettle and big spoon stand always ready for those who at any moment may hunger. There is little to be said about eating in a Seminole household, therefore, except that when its members eat together they make a kettle the center of their group and that much of their eating is done without reference to one another.

AMUSEMENTS.

But one sees the family at home, not only working and sleeping and eating, but also engaged in amusing itself. Especially among the children, various sports are indulged in. I took some trouble to learn what amusements the little Seminole had invented or received. I obtained a list of them which might as well be that of the white man's as of the Indian's child. The Seminole has a doll, i. e., a bundle of rags, a stick with a bit of cloth wrapped about it, or something that serves just as well as this. The children build little houses for their dolls and name them "camps." Boys take their bows and arrows and go into the bushes and kill small birds, and on returning say they have been "turkey-hunting." Children sit around a small piece of land and, sticking blades of grass into the ground, name it a "corn field." They have the game of "hide and seek." They use the dancing rope, manufacture a "see-saw," play "leap frog," and build a "merry-go-round." Carrying a small stick, they say they carry a rifle. I noticed some children at play one day sitting near a dried deer skin, which lay before them stiff and resonant. They had taken from the earth small tubers about an inch in diameter found on the roots of a kind of grass and called "deer-food." Through them they had thrust sharp sticks of the thickness of a match and twice as long, making what we would call "teetotums." These, by a quick twirl between the palms of the hands, were set to spinning on the deer skin. The four children were keeping a dozen or more of these things going. The sport they called "a dance."

I need only add that the relations among the various members of the Indian family in Florida are, as a rule, so well adjusted and observed that home life goes on without discord. The father is beyond question master in his home. To the mother belongs a peculiar domestic importance from her connection with her gens, but both she and her children seek first to know and to do the will of the actual lord of the household. The father is the master without being a tyrant; the mother is a subject without being a slave; the children have not yet learned self-assertion in opposition to their parents: consequently, there is no constraint in family intercourse. The Seminole household is cheerful, its members are mutually confiding, and, in the Indian's way, intimate and affectionate.

THE SEMINOLE GENS.

Of this larger body of kindred, existing, as I could see, in very distinct form among the Seminole, I gained but little definite knowledge. What few facts I secured are here placed on record.

After I was enabled to make my inquiry understood, I sought to learn from my respondent the name of the gens to which each Indian whose name I had received belonged. As the result, I found that the two hundred and eight Seminole now in Florida are divided into the following gentes and in the following numbers:

1. Wind gens	21	7. Bear gens		4
2. Tiger gens	58	8. Wolf gens		1
3. Otter gens	39	9. Alligator gens		1
4. Bird gens	41	Unknown gentes		10
5. Deer gens	18			
6. Snake gens	15	Total		208

I endeavored, also, to learn the name the Indians use for gens or clan, and was told that it is "Po-ha-po-hûm-ko-sin;" the best translation I can give of the name is "Those of one camp or house."

Examining my table to find whether or not the word as translated describes the fact, I notice that, with but one exception, which may not, after all, prove to be an exception, each of the twenty-two camps into which the thirty-seven Seminole families are divided is a camp in which all the persons but the husbands are members of one gens. The camp at Miami is an apparent exception. There Little Tiger, a rather important personage, lives with a number of unmarried relatives. A Wolf has married one of Little Tiger's sisters and lives in the camp, as properly he should. Lately Tiger himself has married an Otter, but, instead of leaving his relatives and going to the camp of his wife's kindred, his wife has taken up her home with his people.

At the Big Cypress Swamp I tried to discover the comparative rank or dignity of the various clans. In reply, I was told by one of the Wind clan that they are graded in the following order. At the northernmost camp, however, another order appears to have been established.

Big Cypress camp.	*Northernmost camp.*
1. The Wind.	1. The Tiger.
2. The Tiger.	2. The Wind.
3. The Otter.	3. The Otter.
4. The Bird.	4. The Bird.
5. The Deer.	5. The Bear.
6. The Snake.	6. The Deer.
7. The Bear.	7. The Buffalo.
8. The Wolf.	8. The Snake.
	9. The Alligator.
	10. The Horned Owl.

This second order was given to me by one of the Bird gens and by one who calls himself distinctively a "Tallahassee" Indian. The Buffalo and the Horned Owl clans seem now to be extinct in Florida, and I am not altogether sure that the Alligator clan also has not disappeared.

The gens is "a group of relatives tracing a common lineage to some remote ancestor. This lineage is traced by some tribes through the mother and by others through the father." "The gens is the grand unit of social organization, and for many purposes is the basis of governmental organization." To the gens belong also certain rights and duties.

Of the characteristics of the gentes of· the Florida Seminole, I know only that a man may not marry a woman of his own clan, that the children belong exclusively to the mother, and that by birth they are members of her own gens. So far as duogamy prevails now among the Florida Indians, I observed that both the wives, in every case, were members of one gens. I understand also that there are certain games in which men selected from gentes as such are the contesting participants.

FELLOWHOOD.

In this connection I may say that if I was understood in my inquiries the Seminole have also the institution of "Fellowhood" among them. Major Powell thus describes this institution : "Two young men agree to be life friends, 'more than brothers,' confiding without reserve each in the other and protecting each the other from all harm."

THE SEMINOLE TRIBE.

TRIBAL ORGANIZATION.

The Florida Seminole, considered as a tribe, have a very imperfect organization. The complete tribal society of the past was much broken up through wars with the United States. These wars having ended in the transfer of nearly the whole of the population to the Indian Territory, the few Indians remaining in Florida were consequently left in a comparatively disorganized condition. There is, however, among these Indians a simple form of government, to which the inhabitants of at least the three southern settlements submit. The people of Cat Fish Lake and Cow Creek settlements live in a large measure independent of or without civil connection with the others. Teup-ko calls his people "Tallahassee Indians." He says that they are not "the same" as the Fish Eating Creek, Big Cypress, and Miami people. I learned, moreover, that the ceremony of the Green Corn Dance may take place at the three last named settlements and not at those of the north. The "Tallahassee Indians" go to Fish Eating Creek if they desire to take part in the festival.

SEAT OF GOVERNMENT.

So far as there is a common seat of government, it is located at Fish Eating Creek, where reside the head chief and big medicine man of the Seminole, Tûs-ta-nûg-ge, and his brother, Hŏs pa-ta-ki, also a medicine man. These two are called the Tûs-ta-nûg-ul-ki, or "great heroes" of the tribe. At this settlement, annually, a council, composed of minor chiefs from the various settlements, meets and passes upon the affairs of the tribe.

TRIBAL OFFICERS.

What the official organization of the tribe is I do not know. My respondent could not tell me. I learned, in addition to what I have just written, only that there are several Indians with official titles, living at each of the settlements, except at the one on Cat Fish Lake. These were classified as follows:

Settlements.	Chief and medicine man.	War chiefs.	Little chiefs.	Medicine men.
Big Cypress Swamp		2	2	1
Miami River		1		1
Fish Eating Creek	1			1
Cow Creek				2
Total	1	3	2	5

NAME OF TRIBE.

I made several efforts to discover the tribal name by which these Indians now designate themselves. The name Seminole they reject. In their own language it means "a wanderer," and, when used as a term of reproach, "a coward." Ko-nip-ha-tco said, "Me no Sem-ai-no-le; Seminole cow, Seminole deer, Seminole rabbit; me no Seminole. Indians gone Arkansas Seminole." He meant that timidity and flight from danger are "Seminole" qualities, and that the Indians who had gone west at the bidding of the Government were the true renegades. This same Indian informed me that the people south of the Caloosahatchie River, at Miami and the Big Cypress Swamp call themselves "Kän-yuk-sa Is-ti-tca-ti," i. e., "Kän-yuk-sa red men." Kän-yuk-sa is their word for what we know as Florida. It is composed of I-kan-a, "ground," and I-yuk-sa, "point" or "tip," i. e., point of ground, or peninsula. At the northern camps the name appropriate to the people there, they say, is "Tallahassee Indians."

CHAPTER III.

SEMINOLE TRIBAL LIFE.

We may now look at the life of the Seminole in its broader relations to the tribal organization. Some light has already been thrown on this subject by the preceding descriptions of the personal characteristics and social relations of these Indians. But there are other matters to be considered, as, for example, industries, arts, religion, and the like.

INDUSTRIES.

AGRICULTURE.

Prominent among the industries is agriculture. The Florida Indians have brought one hundred or more acres of excellent land under a rude sort of cultivation. To each family belong, by right of use and agree-ment with other Indians, fields of from one to four acres in extent. The only agricultural implement they have is the single bladed hoe com-mon on the southern plantation. However, nothing more than this is required.

Soil.— The ground they select is generally in the interiors of the rich hammocks which abound in the swamps and prairies of Southern Flor-ida. There, with a soil unsurpassed in fertility and needing only to be cleared of trees, vines, underbrush, &c., one has but to plant corn, sweet potatoes, melons, or any thing else suited to the climate, and keep weeds from the growing vegetation, that he may gather a manifold re-turn. The soil is wholly without gravel, stones, or rocks. It is soft, black, and very fertile. To what extent the Indians carry agriculture I do not know. I am under the impression, however, that they do not attempt to grow enough to provide much against the future. But, as they have no season in the year wholly unproductive and for which they must make special provision, their improvidence is not followed by serious consequences.

Corn.— The chief product of their agriculture is corn. This becomes edible in the months of May and June and at this time it is eaten in great quantities. Then it is that the annual festival called the " Green Corn Dance" is celebrated. When the corn ripens, a quantity of it is laid aside and gradually used in the form of hominy and of what I heard described as an "exceedingly beautiful meal, white as the finest wheat flour." This meal is produced by a slow and tedious process. The corn is hulled and the germ cut out, so that there is only a pure white residue. This is then reduced by mortar and pestle to an almost impalpable dust. From this flour a cake is made, which is said to be very pleasant to the taste.

Sugar cane.—Another product of their agriculture is the sugar cane. In growing this they are the producers of perhaps the finest sugar cane grown in America; but they are not wise enough to make it a source of profit to themselves. It seems to be cultivated more as a passing luxury. It was at "Old Tommy's" sugar field I met the forty-eight of the people of the Big Cypress Swamp settlement already mentioned. They had left their homes that they might have a pleasuring for a few weeks together, "camping out" and making and eating sirup. The cane which had been grown there was the largest I or my companion, Capt. F. A. Hendry, of Myers, had ever seen. It was two inches or more in diameter, and, as we guessed, seventeen feet or more in length. To obtain the sirup the Indians had constructed two rude mills, the cylinders of which, however, were so loosely adjusted that full half the juice was lost in the process of crushing the cane. The juice was caught in various kinds of iron and tin vessels, kettles, pails, and cans, and after having been strained was boiled until the proper consistency was reached.

Fig. 68. Sugar cane crusher.

At the time we were at the camp quite a quantity of the sirup had been made. It stood around the boiling place in kettles, large and small, and in cans bearing the labels of well known Boston and New York packers, which had been purchased at Myers. Of special interest to me was a platform near the boiling place, on which lay several deer skins, that had been taken as nearly whole as possible from the bodies of the animals, and utilized as holders of the sirup. They were filled with the sweet stuff, and the ground beneath was well covered by a slow leakage from them. "Key West Billy" offered me some of the cane juice to drink. It was clean looking and served in a silver gold lined cup of spotless brilliancy. It made a welcome and delicious drink. I tasted some of the sirup also, eating it Indian fashion, i. e., I pared some of their small boiled wild potatoes and, dipping them into the sweet liquid, ate them. The potato itself tastes somewhat like a boiled chestnut.

The sugar cane mill was a poor imitation of a machine the Indians had seen among the whites. Its cylinders were made of live oak; the driving cogs were cut from a much harder wood, the mastic, I was told; and these were so loosely set into the cylinders that I could take them out with thumb and forefinger. (Fig. 68.)

It is not necessary to speak in particular of the culture of sweet potatoes, beans, melons, &c. At best it is very primitive. It is, however, deserving of mention that the Seminole have around their houses at least a thousand banana plants. When it is remembered that a hundred bananas are not an overlarge yield for one plant, it is seen how well off, so far as this fruit is concerned, these Indians are.

HUNTING.

Next in importance as an industry of the tribe (if it may be so called) is hunting. Southern Florida abounds in game and the Indians have only to seek in order to find it. For this purpose they use the rifle. The bow and arrow are no longer used for hunting purposes except by the smaller children. The rifles are almost all the long, heavy, small bore "Kentucky" rifle. This is economical of powder and lead, and for this reason is preferred by many to even the modern improved weapons which carry fixed ammunition. The Seminole sees the white man so seldom and lives so far from trading posts that he is not willing to be confined to the use of the prepared cartridge.

A few breech loading rifles are owned in the tribe. The shot gun is much disliked by the Seminole. There is only one among them, and that is a combination of shot gun with rifle. I made a careful count of their fire arms, and found that they own, of "Kentucky" rifles, 63; breech loading rifles, 8; shot gun and rifle, 1; revolvers, 2—total, 74.

Methods of hunting.—The Seminole always hunt their game on foot. They can approach a deer to within sixty yards by their method of rapidly nearing him while he is feeding, and standing perfectly still when he raises his head. They say that they are able to discover by certain movements on the part of the deer when the head is about to be lifted. They stand side to the animal. They believe that they can thus deceive the deer, appearing to them as stumps or trees. They lure turkeys within shooting distance by an imitation of the calls of the bird. They leave small game, such as birds, to the children. One day, while some of our party were walking near Horse Creek with Ka-tca-la-ni, a covey of quail whirred out of the grass. By a quick jerk the Indian threw his ramrod among the birds and killed one. He appeared to regard this feat as neither accidental nor remarkable.

I sought to discover how many deer the Seminole annually kill, but could get no number which I can call trustworthy. I venture twenty-five hundred as somewhere near a correct estimate.

Otter hunting is another of the Seminole industries. This animal has been pursued with the rifle and with the bow and arrow. Lately the Indians have heard of the trap. When we left Horse Creek, a request was made by one of them to our guide to purchase for him six otter traps for use in the Cat Fish Lake camp.

FISHING.

Fishing is also a profitable industry. For this the hook and line are often used; some also use the spoon hook. But it is a common practice among them to kill the fish with bow and arrow, and in this they are quite skillful. One morning some boys brought me a bass, weighing perhaps six pounds, which one of them had shot with an arrow.

STOCK RAISING.

Stock raising, in a small way, may be called a Seminole industry. I found that at least fifty cattle, and probably more, are owned by members of the tribe and that the Seminole probably possess a thousand swine and five hundred chickens. The latter are of an excellent breed. At Cat Fish Lake an unusual interest in horses seems now to be developing. I found there twenty horses. I was told that there are twelve horses at Fish Eating Creek, and I judge that between thirty-five and forty of these animals are now in possession of the tribe.

KOONTI.

The unique industry, in the more limited sense of the word, of the Seminole is the making of the Koonti flour. Koonti is a root containing a large percentage of starch. It is said to yield a starch equal to that of the best Bermuda arrowroot. White men call it the " Indian bread root," and lately its worth as an article of commerce has been recognized by the whites. There are now at least two factories in operation in Southern Florida in which the Koonti is made into a flour for the white man's market. I was at one such factory at Miami and saw another near Orlando. I ate of a Koonti pudding at Miami, and can say that, as it was there prepared and served with milk and guava jelly, it was delicious. As might be supposed, the Koonti industry, as carried on by the whites, produces a far finer flour than that which the Indians manufacture. The Indian process, as I watched it at Horse Creek, was this: The roots were gathered, the earth was washed from them, and they were laid in heaps near the " Koonti log."

The Koonti log, so called, was the trunk of a large pine tree, in which a number of holes, about nine inches square at the top, their sides

sloping downward to a point, had been cut side by side.   Each of these
holes was the property of some one of the squaws or of the children of

FIG. 69. Koonti log.

the camp.   For each of the holes, which were to serve as mortars, a
pestle made of some hard wood had been furnished.   (Fig. 69.)

The first step in the process was to reduce the washed Koonti to a
kind of pulp.   This was done by chopping it into small pieces and

FIG. 70. Koonti pestles.

filling with it one of the mortars and pounding it with a pestle.   The
contents of the mortar were then laid upon a small platform.   Each
worker had a platform.   When a sufficient quantity of the root had
been pounded the whole mass was taken to the creek near by and thoroughly saturated with water in a vessel made of bark.

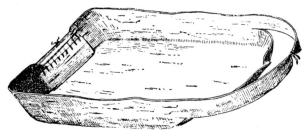

FIG. 71. Koonti mash vessel.

The pulp was then washed in a straining cloth, the starch of the Koonti draining into a deer hide suspended below.

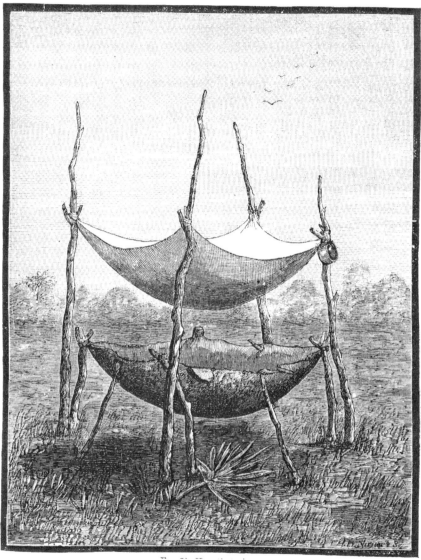

FIG. 72. Koonti strainer.

When the starch had been thoroughly washed from the mass the latter was thrown away, and the starchy sediment in the water in the deer skin left to ferment. After some days the sediment was taken from the water and spread upon palmetto leaves to dry. When dried, it was a yellowish white flour, ready for use. In the factory at Miami substantially this process is followed, the chief variation from it being that the

Koonti is passed through several successive fermentations, thereby making it purer and whiter than the Indian product. Improved appliances for the manufacture are used by the white man.

The Koonti bread, as I saw it among the Indians, was of a bright orange color, and rather insipid, though not unpleasant to the taste. It was saltless. Its yellow color was owing to the fact that the flour had had but one fermentation.

INDUSTRIAL STATISTICS.

The following is a summary of the results of the industries now engaged in by the Florida Indians. It shows what is approximately true of these at the present time:

Acres under cultivation		100
Corn raised	bushels..	500
Sugar cane	gallons..	1,500
Cattle	number owned..	50
Swine	do....	1,000
Chickens	do....	500
Horses	do....	35
Koonti	bushels..	5,000
Sweet potatoes	do....	.....
Melons	number..	3,000

ARTS.

INDUSTRIAL ARTS.

In reference to the way in which the Seminole Indians have met necessities for invention and have expressed the artistic impulse, I found little to add to what I have already placed on record.

Utensils and implements.—The proximity of this people to the Europeans for the last three centuries, while it has not led them to adopt the white man's civilization in matters of government, religion, language, manners, and customs, has, nevertheless, induced them to appropriate for their own use some of the utensils, implements, weapons, &c., of the strangers. For example, it was easy for the ancestors of these Indians to see that the iron kettle of the white man was better in every way than their own earthenware pots. Gradually, therefore, the art of making pottery died out among them, and now, as I believe, there is no pottery whatever in use among the Florida Indians. They neither make nor purchase it. They no longer buy even small articles of earthenware, preferring tin instead. Iron implements likewise have supplanted those made of stone. Even their word for stone, "Tcat-to," has been applied to iron. They purchase hoes, hunting knives, hatchets, axes, and, for special use in their homes, knives nearly two feet in length. With these long knives they dress timber, chop meat, etc.

Weapons.—They continue the use of the bow and arrow, but no longer for the purposes of war, or, by the adults, for the purposes of hunting.

The rifle serves them much better. It seems to be customary for every male in the tribe over twelve years of age to provide himself with a rifle. The bow, as now made, is a single piece of mulberry or other elastic wood and is from four to six feet in length; the bowstring is made of twisted deer rawhide; the arrows are of cane and of hard wood and vary in length from two to four feet; they are, as a rule, tipped with a sharp conical roll of sheet iron. The skill of the young men in the use of the bow and arrow is remarkable.

Weaving and basket making.—The Seminole are not now weavers. Their few wants for clothing and bedding are supplied by fabrics manufactured by white men. They are in a small way, however, basket makers. From the swamp cane, and sometimes from the covering of the stalk of the fan palmetto, they manufacture flat baskets and sieves for domestic service.

Uses of the palmetto.—In this connection I call attention to the inestimable value of the palmetto tree to the Florida Indians. From the trunk of the tree the frames and platforms of their houses are made; of its leaves durable water tight roofs are made for the houses; with the leaves their lodges are covered and beds protecting the body from the dampness of the ground are made; the tough fiber which lies between the stems of the leaves and the bark furnishes them with material from which they make twine and rope of great strength and from which they could, were it necessary, weave cloth for clothing; the tender new growth at the top of the tree is a very nutritious and palatable article of food, to be eaten either raw or baked; its taste is somewhat like that of the chestnut; its texture is crisp like that of our celery stalk.

Mortar and pestle.—The home made mortar and pestle has not yet been supplanted by any utensil furnished by the trader. This is still the best mill they have in which to grind their corn. The mortar is made from a log of live oak (?) wood, ordinarily about two feet in length and from fifteen to twenty inches in diameter. One end of the log is hollowed out to quite a depth, and in this, by the hammering of a pestle made of mastic wood, the corn is reduced to hominy or to the impalpable flour of which I have spoken. (Fig. 73.)

FIG. 73. Mortar and pestle.

Canoe making.—Canoe making is still one of their industrial arts, the canoe being their chief means of transportation. The Indian settlements are all so situated that the inhabitants of one can reach those of the others by water. The canoe is what is known as a "dugout," made from the cypress log.

Fire making.—The art of fire making by simple friction is now, I be- lieve, neglected among the Seminole, unless at the starting of the sacred fire for the Green Corn Dance. A fire is now kindled either by the common Ma-tci (matches) of the civilized man or by steel and flint, powder and paper. "Tom Tiger" showed me how he builds a fire when away from home. He held, crumpled between the thumb and fore- finger of the left hand, a bit of paper. In the folds of the paper he poured from his powder horn a small quantity of gunpowder. Close beside the paper he held also a piece of flint. Striking this flint with a bit of steel and at the same time giving to the left hand a quick up- ward movement, he ignited the powder and paper. From this he soon made a fire among the pitch pine chippings he had previously prepared.

Preparation of skins.—I did not learn just how the Indians dress deer skins, but I observed that they had in use and for sale the dried skin, with the hair of the animal left on it; the bright yellow buckskin, very soft and strong; and also the dark red buckskin, which evidently had passed, in part of its preparation, through smoke. I was told that the brains of the animal serve an important use in the skin dressing proc- ess. The accompanying sketch shows a simple frame in use for stretch- ing and drying the skin. (Fig. 74.)

FIG. 74. Hide stretcher.

ORNAMENTAL ARTS.

In my search for evidence of the working of the art instinct proper, i. e., in ornamental or fine art, I found but little to add to what has been already said. I saw but few attempts at ornamentation beyond those made on the person and on clothing. Houses, canoes, utensils, implements, weapons, were almost all without carving or painting. In fact, the only carving I noticed in the Indian country was on a pine tree near Myers. It was a rude outline of the head of a bull. The local report is that when the white men began to send their cattle south of the Caloosahatchie River the Indians marked this tree with this sign. The only painting I saw was the rude representation of a man, upon the shaft of one of the pestles used at the Koonti log at Horse Creek. It was made by one of the girls for her own amusement.

I have already spoken of the art of making silver ornaments.

Music.—Music, as far as I could discover, is but little in use among the Seminole. Their festivals are few; so few that the songs of the fathers have mostly been forgotten. They have songs for the Green Corn Dance; they have lullabys; and there is a doleful song they sing in praise of drink, which is occasionally heard when the white man has sold Indians whisky on coming to town. Knowing the motive of the song, I thought the tune stupid and maudlin. Without pretending to reproduce it exactly, I remember it as something like this:

My precious drink, I fondly love thee. Standing I take thee. And walk until morning. Yo-wan-ha-de.

I give a free translation of the Indian words and an approximation to the tune. The last note in this, as in the lullaby I noted above, is unmusical and staccato.

RELIGION.

I could learn but little of the religious faiths and practices existing among the Florida Indians. I was struck, however, in making my investigations, by the evident influence Christian teaching has had upon the native faith. How far it has penetrated the inherited thought of the Indian I do not know. But, in talking with Ko-nip-ha-tco, he told me that his people believe that the Koonti root was a gift from God; that long ago the "Great Spirit" sent Jesus Christ to the earth with the precious plant, and that Jesus had descended upon the world at Cape Florida and there given the Koonti to "the red men." In reference to this tradition, it is to be remembered that during the seventeenth century the Spaniards had vigorous missions among the Florida Indians. Doubtless it was from these that certain Christian names and beliefs now traceable among the Seminole found way into the savage creed and ritual.

I attempted several times to obtain from my interpreter a statement of the religious beliefs he had received from his people. I cannot affirm with confidence that success followed my efforts.

He told me that his people believe in a "Great Spirit," whose name is His-a-kit-a-mis i. This word, I have good reason to believe, means "the master of breath." The Seminole for breath is His-a-kit-a.

I cannot be sure that Ko-nip-ha-tco knew anything of what I meant by the word "spirit." I tried to convey my meaning to him, but I think I failed. He told me that the place to which Indians go after death is called "Po-ya-fi-tsa" and that the Indians who have died are the Pi-ya-fits-ul-ki, or "the people of Po-ya-fi-tsa." That was our nearest understanding of the word "spirit" or "soul."

MORTUARY CUSTOMS.

As the Seminole mortuary customs are closely connected with their religious beliefs, it will be in place to record here what I learned of them. The description refers particularly to the death and burial of a child.

The preparation for burial began as soon as death had taken place. The body was clad in a new shirt, a new handkerchief being tied about the neck and another around the head. A spot of red paint was placed on the right cheek and one of black upon the left. The body was laid face upwards. In the left hand, together with a bit of burnt wood, a small bow about twelve inches in length was placed, the hand lying naturally over the middle of the body. Across the bow, held by the right hand, was laid an arrow, slightly drawn. During these preparations, the women loudly lamented, with hair disheveled. At the same time some men had selected a place for the burial and made the grave in

FIG. 75. Seminole bier.

this manner: Two palmetto logs of proper size were split. The four pieces were then firmly placed on edge, in the shape of an oblong box, lengthwise east and west. In this box a floor was laid, and over this a blanket was spread. Two men, at next sunrise, carried the body from

the camp to the place of burial, the body being suspended at feet
thighs, back, an d neck from a long pole (Fig. 75). The relatives fol.
lowed. In the grave, which is called "To hŏp-ki"—a word used by
the Seminole for "stockade," or "fort," also, the body was then laid
the feet to the east. A blanket was then carefully wrapped around the
body. Over this palmetto leaves were placed and the grave was tightly
closed by a covering of logs. Above the box a roof was then built
Sticks, in the form of an **X**, were driven into the earth across the over-
lying logs; these were connected by a pole, and this structure was covered thickly with palmetto leaves. (Fig. 76.)

Fig. 76. Seminole grave.

The bearers of the body then made a large fire at each end of the "To.
hŏp ki." With this the ceremony at the grave ended and all returned
to the camp. During that day and for three days thereafter the relatives remained at home and refrained from work. The fires at the grave
were renewed at sunset by those who had made them, and after nightfall torches were there waved in the air, that "the bad birds of the
night" might not get at the Indian lying in his grave. The renewal of
the fires and waving of the torches were repeated three days. The fourth
day the fires were allowed to die out. Throughout the camp "medicine"
had been sprinkled at sunset for three days. On the fourth day it was
said that the Indian "had gone." From that time the mourning ceased
and the members of the family returned to their usual occupations.

The interpretation of the ceremonies just mentioned, as given me, is
this: The Indian was laid in his grave to remain there, it was believed,
only until the fourth day. The fires at head and feet, as well as the
waving of the torches, were to guard him from the approach of "evil
birds" who would harm him. His feet were placed toward the east,
that when he arose to go to the skies he might go straight to the sky

path, which commenced at the place of the sun's rising; that were he
laid with the feet in any other direction he would not know when he rose
what path to take and he would be lost in the darkness. He had with
him his bow and arrow, that he might procure food on his way. The
piece of burnt wood in his hand was to protect him from the "bad
birds" while he was on his skyward journey. These "evil birds" are
called Ta-lak-i-çlak-o. The last rite paid to the Seminole dead is at
the end of four moons. At that time the relatives go to the To-hŏp-ki
and cut from around it the overgrowing grass. A widow lives with
disheveled hair for the first twelve moons of her widowhood.

GREEN CORN DANCE.

The one institution at present in which the religious beliefs of the
Seminole find special expression is what is called the "Green Corn
Dance." It is the occasion for an annual purification and rejoicing. I
could get no satisfactory description of the festival. No white man, so
I was told, has seen it, and the only Indian I met who could in any manner speak English made but an imperfect attempt to describe it. In
fact, he seemed unwilling to talk about it. He told me, however, that
as the season for holding the festival approaches the medicine men
assemble and, through their ceremonies, decide when it shall take
place, and, if I caught his meaning, determine also how long the dance
shall continue. Others, on the contrary, told me that the dance is
always continued for four days.

Fifteen days previous to the festival heralds are sent from the lodge
of the medicine men to give notice to all the camps of the day when the
dance will commence. Small sticks are thereupon hung up in each
camp, representing the number of days between that date and the day
of the beginning of the dance. With the passing of each day one of
these sticks is thrown away. The day the last one is cast aside the families go to the appointed place. At the dancing ground they find the
selected space arranged as in the accompanying diagram (Fig. 77).

The evening of the first day the ceremony of taking the "Black
Drink," Pa-sa-is-kit-a, is endured. This drink was described to me as
having both a nauseating smell and taste. It is probably a mixture
similar to that used by the Creek in the last century at a like ceremony. It acts as both an emetic and a cathartic, and it is believed
among the Indians that unless one drinks of it he will be sick at some
time in the year, and besides that he cannot safely eat of the green corn
of the feast. During the drinking the dance begins and proceeds; in
it the medicine men join.

At that time the Medicine Song is sung. My Indian would not repeat this song for me. He declared that any one who sings the Medicine Song, except at the Green Corn Dance or as a medicine man,
will certainly meet with some harm. That night, after the "Black
Drink" has had its effect, the Indians sleep. The next morning they

eat of the green corn. The day following is one of fasting, but the next day is one of great feasting, "Hom-pi-ta-çlak-o," in which "Indian eat all time," "Hom-pis-yak-i-ta."

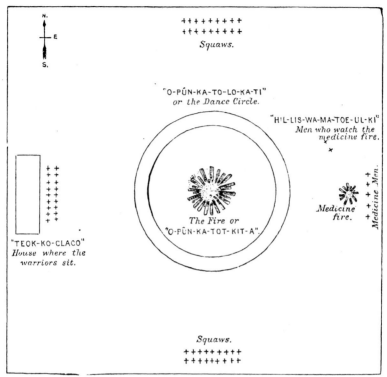

FIG. 77. Green Corn Dance.

USE OF MEDICINES.

Concerning the use by the Indians of medicine against sickness, I learned only that they are in the habit of taking various herbs for their ailments. What part incantation or sorcery plays in the healing of disease I do not know. Nor did I learn what the Indians think of the origin and effects of dreams. Me-le told me that he knows of a plant the leaves of which, eaten, will cure the bite of a rattlesnake, and that he knows also of a plant which is an antidote to the noxious effects of the poison ivy or so-called poison oak.

GENERAL OBSERVATIONS.

I close this chapter by putting upon record a few general observations, as an aid to future investigation into Seminole life.

STANDARD OF VALUE.

The standard of value among the Florida Indians is now taken from the currency of the United States. The unit they seem to have adopted, at least at the Big Cypress Swamp settlement, is twenty-five cents, which they call "Kau-cat-ka-hum-kin" (literally, "one mark on the ground"). At Miami a trader keeps his accounts with the Indians in single marks or pencil strokes. For example, an Indian brings to him buck skins, for which the trader allows twelve "chalks." The Indian, not wishing then to purchase anything, receives a piece of paper marked in this way:

"IIII–IIII–IIII.
J. W. E. owes Little Tiger $3."

At his next visit the Indian may buy five "marks" worth of goods The trader then takes the paper and returns it to Little Tiger changed as follows:

"IIII–III.
J. W. E. owes Little Tiger
$1.75."

Thus the account is kept until all the "marks" are crossed off, when the trader takes the paper into his own possession. The value of the purchases made at Miami by the Indians, I was informed, is annually about $2,000. This is, however, an amount larger than would be the average for the rest of the tribe, for the Miami Indians do a considerable business in the barter and sale of ornamental plumage.

What the primitive standard of value among the Seminole was is suggested to me by their word for money, "Tcat-to Ko-na-wa." "Ko-na-wa" means beads, and "Tcat-to," while it is the name for iron and metal, is also the name for stone. "Tcat-to" probably originally meant stone. Tcat-to Ko-na-wa (i. e., stone beads) was, then, the primitive money. With "Hat-ki," or white, added, the word means silver; with "La-ni," or yellow, added, it means gold. For greenbacks they use the words "Nak-ho-tsi Tcat-to Ko-na-wa," which is, literally, "paper stone beads."

Their methods of measuring are now, probably, those of the white man. I questioned my respondent closely, but could gain no light upon the terms he used as equivalents for our measurements.

DIVISIONS OF TIME.

I also gained but little knowledge of their divisions of time. They have the year, the name for which is the same as that used for summer, and in their year are twelve months, designated, respectively:

1. Çla-fŭts-u-tsi, Little Winter.
2. Ho-ta-li-ha-si, Wind Moon.
3. Ho-ta-li-ha-si-çlak-o, Big Wind Moon.
4. Ki-ha-su-tsi, Little Mulberry Moon.
5. Ki-ha-si-çlak-o, Big Mulberry Moon.
6. Ka-tco-ha-si.
7. Hai-yu-tsi.
8. Hai-yu-tsi-çlak-o.
9. O-ta-wŭs-ku-tsi.
10. O-ta-wŭs-ka-çlak-o.
11. I-ho-li.
12. Çla-fo-çlak-o, Big Winter.

I suppose that the spelling of these words could be improved, but I reproduce them phonetically as nearly as I can, not making what to me would be desirable corrections. The months appear to be divided simply into days, and these are, in part at least, numbered by reference to successive positions of the moon at sunset. When I asked Täl-la-häs-ke how long he would stay at his present camp, he made reply by pointing to the new moon in the west and sweeping his hand from west to east to where the moon would be when he should go home. He meant to answer, about ten days thence. The day is divided by terms descriptive of the positions of the sun in the sky from dawn to sunset.

NUMERATION.

The Florida Indians can count, by their system, indefinitely. Their system of numeration is quinary, as will appear from the following list:

1. Hŭm-kin.		7. *Ko-lo*-pa-kin.
2. Ho-*ko-lin*.		8. *Tci-na*-pa-kin.
3. To-*tci-nin*.		9. *Os-ta*-pa-kin.
4. *Os-tin*.		10. Pa-lin.
5. Tsaq-ke-pin.		11. Pa-lin-hŭm-kin, *i. e.*, ten one, &c.
6. I-pa-kin.		20. Pa-li-ho-ko-lin, i. e., two tens.

As a guide towards a knowledge of the primitive manner of counting the method used by an old man in his intercourse with me will serve. He wished to count eight. He first placed the thumb of the right hand upon the little finger of the left, then the right forefinger upon the next left hand finger, then the thumb on the next finger, and the fore-finger on the next, and then the thumb upon the thumb; leaving now the thumb of the right hand resting upon the thumb of the left, he counted the remaining numbers on the right hand, using for this pur-pose the fore and middle fingers of the left; finally he shut the fourth and little fingers of the right hand down upon its palm, and raising his hands, thumbs touching, the counted fingers outspread, he showed me eight as the number of horses of which I had made inquiry.

SENSE OF COLOR

Concerning the sense of color among these Indians, I found that my informant at least possessed it to only a very limited degree. Black and white were clear to his sight, and for these he had appropriate names. Also for brown, which was to him a "yellow black," and for gray, which was a "white black." For some other colors his perception was distinct and the names he used proper. But a name for blue he applied to many other colors, shading from violet to green. A name for red followed a succession of colors all the way from scarlet to pink. A name for yellow he applied to dark orange and thence to a list of colors through to yellow's lightest and most delicate tint. I thought that at one time I had found him making a clear distinction between green and blue, but as I examined further I was never certain that he would not exchange the names when asked about one or the other color.

EDUCATION.

The feeling of the tribe is antagonistic to even such primary education as reading, writing, and calculation. About ten years ago an attempt, the only attempt in modern times, to establish schools among them was made by Rev. Mr. Frost, now at Myers, Fla. He did not succeed.

SLAVERY.

By reference to the population table, it will be noticed that there are three negroes and seven persons of mixed breed among the Seminole. It has been said that these negroes were slaves and are still held as slaves by the Indians. I saw nothing and could not hear of anything to justify this statement. One Indian is, I know, married to a negress, and the two negresses in the tribe live apparently on terms of perfect equality with the other women. Me-le goes and comes as he sees fit. No one attempts to control his movements. It may be that long ago the Florida Indians held negroes as slaves, but my impression is to the contrary. The Florida Indians, I think, rather offered a place of refuge for fugitive bondmen and gradually made them members of their tribe.

HEALTH.

In the introduction to this report I said that the health of the Seminole is good. As confirming this statement, I found that the deaths during the past year had been very few. I had trustworthy information concerning the deaths of only four persons. One of these deaths was of an old woman, O-pa-ka, at the Fish Eating Creek settlement; another was of Täl-la-häs-ke's wife, at Cat Fish Lake settlement; another was of a sister of Täl-la-häs-ke; and the last was of a child, at Cow Creek settlement. At the Big Cypress Swamp settlement I was assured that no deaths had occurred either there or at Miami during the year. On the contrary, however, I was told by some white people at Miami that several children had died at the Indian camp near there in the year past. Täl-la-häs-ke said to me, "Twenty moons ago, heap pickaninnies die!" And I was informed by others that about two years before there had been considerable fatality among children, as the consequence of a sort of epidemic at one of the northern camps. Admitting the correctness of these reports, I have no reason to modify my general statement that the health of the Seminole is good and that they are certainly increasing their number. Their appearance indicates excellent health and their environment is in their favor.

CHAPTER IV.

ENVIRONMENT OF THE SEMINOLE.

NATURE.

Southern Florida, the region to which most of the Seminole have been driven by the advances of civilization, is, taken all in all, unlike any other part of our country. In climate it is subtropical; in character of soil it shows a contrast of comparative barrenness and abounding fertility; and in topography it is a plain, with hardly any perceptible natural elevations or depressions. The following description, based upon the notes of my journey to the Big Cypress Swamp, indicates the character of the country generally. I left Myers, on the Caloosahatchie River, a small settlement composed principally of cattlemen, one morning in the month of February. Even in February the sun was so hot that clothing was a burden. As we started upon our journey, which was to be for a distance of sixty miles or more, my attention was called to the fact that the harness of the horse attached to my buggy was without the breeching. I was told that this part of the harness would not be needed, so level should we find the country. Our way, soon after leaving the main street of Myers, entered pine woods. The soil across which we traveled at first was a dry, dazzling white sand, over which was scattered a growth of dwarf palmetto. The pine trees were not near enough together to shade us from the fierce sun. This sparseness of growth, and comparative absence of shade, is one marked characteristic of Florida's pine woods. Through this thin forest we drove all the day. The monotonous scenery was unchanged except that at a short distance from Myers it was broken by swamps and ponds. So far as the appearance of the country around us indicated, we could not tell whether we were two miles or twenty from our starting point. Nearly half our way during the first day lay through water, and yet we were in the midst of what is called the winter "dry season." The water took the shape here of a swamp and there of a pond, but where the swamp or the pond began or ended it was scarcely possible to tell. one passed by almost imperceptible degrees from dry land to moist and from moist land into pool or marsh. Generally, however, the swamps were filled with a growth of cypress trees. These cypress groups were well defined in the pine woods by the closeness of their growth and the sharpness of the boundary of the clusters. Usually, too, the cypress swamps were surrounded by rims of water grasses. Six miles from Myers we crossed a cypress swamp, in which the water at its greatest depth was from one foot to two feet deep. A wagon road had

been cut through the dense growth of trees, and the trees were covered
with hanging mosses and air plants.

The ponds differed from the swamps only in being treeless. They are
open sheets of water surrounded by bands of greater or less width of
tall grasses. The third day, between 30 and 40 miles from Myers, we
left the pine tree lands and started across what are called in Southern
Florida the "prairies." These are wide stretches covered with grass and
with scrub palmetto and dotted at near intervals with what are called
pine "islands" or "hammocks" and cypress swamps. The pine island
or hammock is a slight elevation of the soil, rising a few inches above
the dead level. The cypress swamp, on the contrary, seems to have its
origin only in a slight depression in the plain. Where there is a ring
of slight depression, inclosing a slight elevation, there is generally a
combination of cypress and pine and oak growth. For perhaps 15 miles
we traveled that third day over this expanse of grass; most of the way
we were in water, among pine islands, skirting cypress swamps and saw-
grass marshes, and being jolted through thick clumps of scrub palmetto.
Before nightfall we reached the district occupied by the Indians, passing there into what is called the "Bad Country," an immense expanse
of submerged land, with here and there islands rising from it, as from
the drier prairies. We had a weird ride that afternoon and night:
Now we passed through saw-grass 5 or 6 feet high and were in water 6 to
20 inches in depth ; then we encircled some impenetrable jungle of vines
and trees, and again we took our way out upon a vast expanse of water
and grass. At but one place in a distance of several miles was it dry
enough for one to step upon the ground without wetting the feet. We
reached that place at nightfall, but found no wood there for making a fire.
We were 4 miles then from any good camping ground. Captain Hendry asked our Indian companion whether he could take us through the
darkness to a place called the "Buck Pens." Ko-nip-ha-tco said he
could. Under his guidance we started in the twilight, the sky covered
with clouds. The night which followed was starless, and soon we were
splashing through a country which, to my eyes, was trackless. There
were visible to me no landmarks. But our Indian, following a trail
made by his own people, about nine o'clock brought us to the object
of our search. A black mass suddenly appeared in the darkness. It
was the pine island we were seeking, the "Buck Pens."

On our journey that day we had crossed a stream, so called, the Ak-
ho-lo-wa-koo-tci. So level is the country, however, and so sluggish the
flow of water there that this river, where we crossed it, was more like
a swamp than a stream. Indeed, in Southern Florida the streams, for
a long distance from what would be called their sources, are more a
succession of swamps than well defined currents confined to channels
by banks. They have no real shores until they are well on their way
towards the ocean.

Beyond the point I reached, on the edge of the Big Cypress Swamp, lie the Everglades proper, a wide district with only deeper water and better defined islands than those which mark the "Bad Country" and the "Devil's Garden" I had entered.

The description I have given refers to that part of the State of Florida lying south of the Caloosahatchee River. It is in this watery prairie and Everglade region that we find the immediate environment of most of the Seminole Indians. Of the surroundings of the Seminole north of the Caloosahatchee there is but little to say in modification of what has already been said. Near the Fish Eating Creek settlement there is a somewhat drier prairie land than that which I have just described. The range of barren sand hills which extends from the north along the middle of Florida to the headwaters of the Kissimmee River ends at Cat Fish Lake. Excepting these modifications, the topography of the whole Indian country of Florida is substantially the same as that which we traversed on the way from Myers into the Big Cypress Swamp and the Everglades.

Over this wide and seeming level of land and water, as I have said, there is a subtropical climate. I visited the Seminole in midwinter; yet, for all that my northern senses could discover, we were in the midst of summer. The few deciduous trees there were having a midyear pause, but trees with dense foliage, flowers, fruit, and growing grass were to be seen everywhere. The temperature was that of a northern June. By night we made our beds on the ground without discomfort from cold, and by day we were under the heat of a summer sun. There was certainly nothing in the climate to make one feel the need of more clothing or shelter than would protect from excessive heat or rain.

Then the abundance of food, both animal and vegetable, obtainable in that region seemed to me to do away with the necessity, on the part of the people living there, for a struggle for existence. As I have already stated, the soil is quite barren over a large part of the district; but, on the other hand, there is also in many places a fertility of soil that cannot be surpassed. Plantings are followed by superabundant harvests, and the hunter is richly rewarded. But I need not repeat what has already been said; it suffices to note that the natural environment of the Seminole is such that ordinary effort serves to supply them, physically, with more than they need.

MAN.

When we consider, in connection with these facts, what I have also before said, that these Indians are in no exceptional danger from wild animals or poisonous reptiles, that they need not specially guard against epidemic disease, and when we remember that they are native to whatever influences might affect injuriously persons from other parts of the country, we can easily see how much more favorably situated for physical prosperity they are than others of their kind. In fact, nature has made physical life so easy to them that their great danger lies in the possible want or decadence of the moral strength needed to maintain them in a vigorous use of their powers. This moral strength to some degree they have, but in large measure it had its origin in and has been preserved by their struggles with man rather than with nature. The wars of their ancestors, extending over nearly two centuries, did the most to make them the brave and proud people they are. It is through the effects of these chiefly that they have been kept from becoming indolent and effeminate. They are now strong, fearless, haughty, and independent. But the near future is to initiate a new epoch in their history, an era in which their career may be the reverse of what it has been. Man is becoming a factor of new importance in their environment. The moving lines of the white population are closing in upon the land of the Seminole. There is no farther retreat to which they can go. It is their impulse to resist the intruders, but some of them are at last becoming wise enough to know that they cannot contend successfully with the white man. It is possible that even their few warriors may make an effort to stay the oncoming hosts, but ultimately they will either perish in the futile attempt or they will have to submit to a civilization which, until now, they have been able to repel and whose injurious accompaniments may degrade and destroy them. Hitherto the white man's influence has been comparatively of no effect except in arousing in the Indian his more violent passions and in exciting him to open hostility. For more than three centuries the European has been face to face with the Florida Indian and the two have never really been friends. Through the seventeenth and eighteenth centuries the peninsula was the scene of frequently renewed warfare. Spaniard, Frenchman, Englishman, and Spaniard, in turn, kept the country in an unsettled state, and when the American Union received the province from Spain, sixty years ago, it received with it, in the tribe of the Seminole, an embittered and determined race of hostile subjects. This people our Government has never been able to conciliate or to conquer. A different Indian policy, or a different administration of it, might have prevented the disastrous wars of the last half century; but, as all know, the Seminole have always lived within our borders as aliens. It is only of late years, and through natural necessities, that any friendly intercourse of white man and Indian has been secured. The Indian has become too weak to contend successfully against his neighbor and the white man has learned enough to refrain from arousing the vindictiveness of the savage. The few white men now on the border line in Florida are, with only some exceptions, cattle dealers or traders seeking barter with the red men. The cattlemen sometimes meet the Indians on the prairies and are friendly with them for the sake of their stock, which often strays into the Seminole country. The other places of contact of the whites and Seminole are the settlements of Myers, Miami, Bartow, Fort Meade, and Tampa, all, however, centers of comparatively small population. To these places, at infrequent intervals, the Indians go for purposes of trade.

The Indians have appropriated for their service some of the products of European civilization, such as weapons, implements, domestic utensils, fabrics for clothing, &c. Mentally, excepting a few religious ideas which they received long ago from the teaching of Spanish missionaries and, in the southern settlements, excepting some few Spanish words, the Seminole have accepted and appropriated practically nothing from the white man. The two peoples remain, as they always have been, separate and independent. Up to the present, therefore, the human environment has had no effect upon the Indians aside from that which has just been noticed, except to arouse them to war and to produce among them war's consequences.

But soon a great and rapid change must take place. The large immigration of a white population into Florida, and especially the attempts at present being made to drain Lake Okeechobee and the Everglades, make it certain, as I have said, that the Seminole is about to enter a future unlike any past he has known. But now that new factors are beginning to direct his career, now that he can no longer retreat, now that he can no longer successfully contend, now that he is to be forced into close, unavoidable contact with men he has known only as enemies, what will he become? If we anger him, he still can do much harm before we can conquer him; but if we seek, by a proper policy, to do him justice, he yet may be made our friend and ally. Already, to the dislike of the old men of the tribe, some young braves show a willingness to break down the ancient barriers between them and our people, and I believe it possible that with encouragement, at a time not far distant, all these Indians may become our friends, forgetting their tragic past in a peaceful and prosperous future.